An Anthology of Short Stories and Verses

To Judy,

Enjoy!

Ted

July 2017

An Anthology of Short Stories and Verses

———

Theodore R. Cromack

ISBN-13: 9781530608317
ISBN-10: 1530608317

Contents

Introduction

"BEN'S ODYSSEY" WAS DEVELOPED AS a part of a larger work, a novel involving the building of the Hoosac Tunnel, in which Ben is a secondary character.

"The Survivors" reflects my interpretation of the effects of military service on many veterans.

"Robin Hoodwink" won second prize in a writing contest sponsored by the now defunct *West County News*. The instruction was to write a short story dealing with agriculture.

"The Shires of Berk" was published in a book by Eber and Wein Publishing, Shrewsbury, Pennsylvania, in 2007.

"It Always Rains for a Funeral" was prompted by a bit of research and an idea for a novel relating to the destruction of the several towns when the Quabbin Reservoir was built.

"Thoughts on Veterans Day" is one of the several pieces resulting from my musings concerning the plight of veterans.

"The Lottery Ticket" was a result of my search for irony in everyday activities by ordinary people whom I see purchasing lottery tickets by the dozens in local convenience stores.

"Center of the Universe" resulted from a memory of a person from my past who reminded me that the sun didn't rise or set; it was the earth that was moving.

"Milking Time" was written much more briefly, responding to a "writing prompt" in one of the writing groups that I attended. The prompt dealt with writing something about your name. I decided to take that little piece and add to it. This is one of the *true* stories in the anthology.

"Passing of a Generation" was written and read at the ceremony celebrating my father's life. Those who knew him will perhaps note the highlights of a life well lived.

"A Day of Golf" represents my favorite pastime wrapped around a common joke among golfers. It was the result of a writing project to prepare a short story to read to the writing group.

"Life on a Silver Wing" was prepared for and read at a celebration of life service for my youngest brother. The title was borrowed from a poem circulated among airmen.

"The Marine" represents what I suspect was a fairly widespread experience during the Vietnam era, the alienation of a son from his father over their interpretation of patriotism. In fact, a less permanent alienation occurred in the family of a friend.

"Lives We Touch" is an admonition to beware of unintended messages.

"The Break-In" was included because of my fondness for mysteries.

"Dreamland" was published in *From a Window*, a poetry anthology by Eber and Wein Publishing, Shrewsbury, Pennsylvania, in 2009. Don't we all have regrets?

"Horse Trading" is the result of some embellishment of a story handed down from my father concerning my grandfather's experience with horse trading.

"Music" seems to be part of everyone's life. There are many aspects to our enjoyment of music. I included it because of my love of music, even if I am not a real musician.

"Compatibility" was written as a "what if" with an ironic twist. It is included only because I enjoy the irony.

"Memories Packed Away" are sometimes better left packed away. I included it because I suspect I am not the only person who won't let go of regrets.

"The Good Samaritan" is a somewhat fictionalized version of a tale my brother tells of his trip home from Illinois when he was in the air force.

"Tempted by the Trail" is an attempt at alliteration and memories of the Arms Academy class of 1945.

"The Golfer" probably doesn't belong in this book. It was an attempt to make a story out of a brief joke. Skip it if you wish.

"I Am the Eagle" was written and included with pride for two young men who earned the rank of Eagle Scout: Nathan Smith and Charles D. Cromack Jr.

"The Eighth Anniversary" was the response to a contest to write about an anniversary. I elected to reach for a different kind of anniversary, and it is included because it represents settings similar to some of those from my life.

"If I Ever Get Old" was written as a joke. A staff member at the local senior center asked if I didn't want to participate in the center's activities, and I responded that I would if I ever got old (being only eighty-four.)

"Coming Home" returns again to the theme of the veteran, this one a true hero, even if a fictionalized one.

"All Living Things Are Born to Die" was prepared for and read at the memorial service for my son-in-law, John Allan. It is a similar theme reflected in some of my other writings.

"A Brief History of the Shelburne Church" is a brief summary that I put together from a number of sources. I present it as a true story but cannot confirm some of the anecdotes.

"A Father's Thoughts" was written in hopes that my sons would realize how proud I am of them. Each has accomplished much in his own way. (Published in the *Annual Who's Who in Poetry* by Eber and Wein, publishers, Shrewsbury, Pennsylvania, 2014.)

"Homeless" was initially a response to a writing prompt in a writing group. It was then expanded and carries through one of my favorite themes of veterans and their plight.

"Birthdays" was the result of an assignment in a writing group. It also reflects my obsession with the changing seasons.

"Valentine's Day" is also the result of an assignment in a writing group. I continually search, especially in short stories, for irony.

"The Optimist" is a rigidly metered poem with nine syllables in each line.

"The Interview" depicts a situation where this writer might be an old man, but he is also an impatient driver.

Ben's Odyssey

———————

BENJAMIN GOT A SEVERE LECTURE from his mother when he was thirteen. When he was fourteen, Mr. Gottlieb grabbed him with a pocketful of his fruit, and he got a lecture accompanied by a cuff and size eleven from Patrolman O'Malley. The judge gave him a lecture and a warning when he was nabbed running numbers at age fifteen. When he appeared before the judge at sixteen, he was given another option.

This was life in Brooklyn for a small boy with a big mouth and a funny name. Benjamin, named for some historical figure before he was born, reached his full height of five feet six at age fifteen. What he lacked in height, however, he made up for in tenacity. He was described by one of his classmates—he had a few during his occasional school attendance—as a boy who would "take no shit" from anyone.

On the streets of Brooklyn, he held his own among the gangs of youth who roamed around terrorizing the merchants and other gangs. Hardly a week went by that he did not return home with a split lip or black eye and skinned knuckles.

Benjamin Vanelli, also known as Benny the Wop, had begun a life on the street in Brooklyn with several disadvantages and perhaps one advantage. He was bright.

Benjamin's father had disappeared shortly after the birth of his son. Mrs. Vanelli worked as a seamstress in a dress factory in order to keep a roof over their heads and food on the table. She cared for Benjamin until she passed away when he was seven. From that time on, Benjamin was a ward of the streets. From time to time, he attended school until he became bored, and then he joined other truants who hung around the streets until a merchant shooed them off or a patrol officer moved them along. His education consisted of learning to steal from anyone whose head turned for a moment and to pick pockets whenever he had a chance. Eventually he worked his way up to running numbers for the mob.

Benny was street-smart by the age of eight. When school let out in the afternoon, he was expected to go home and behave himself. He seldom did.

By the age of ten, Benny could swipe a piece of fruit or a tin of tobacco without being caught nine out of ten times. By the age of twelve, he had come to the attention of Gino Antonelli, the local bookmaker, who admired both his self-confidence and his fleetness.

A raid by the NYPD on a Saturday afternoon at the numbers shop in the back room of Kelly's bar ended Benjamin's career as a hoodlum. They brought in six men and three boys and had all of the evidence cold to lock them up.

"Gotcha' now, ye little punk!" said O'Malley with a grin. "I been watchin' ye for a long time. I knew ye was a punk fer years and knew ye'd end up bein' trouble."

"Stuff it, O'Mally!" Benjamin responded, for which he received a blow upside the head.

"Benjamin, do you see that gentleman in the blue uniform of Mr. Lincoln's army standing in the back of the courtroom?" the judge asked.

"Yes, sir, I do."

"You have two choices. Either go back and tell that man that you wish to join Mr. Lincoln's army or go to jail. This is the second time that you have come into my court, and I want it to be the last. Which do you wish to choose, the army or the jail?"

"I'll choose the army, judge." It took him only a few seconds to decide that it was not only a reasonable choice, but it was what he really wanted to do anyway.

"Then let me see you go back there and join that sergeant. I think it was a wise choice, and you seem smart enough to take advantage of this opportunity. May God watch over you."

In 1862, Benjamin Vanelli, age sixteen, became Private Vanelli of the Union army.

"You can't shoot for shit, Vanelli! You couldn't hit the broad side of a barn from twenty feet away. What good are ye?"

"I can shove this shiv into yer gullet, Sarge," Vanelli responded in a menacing voice.

"Ye'll not get close enough to a Johnny Reb to stick him with that pig sticker though. Ye'll have to learn to shoot,"

Sergeant Robbins replied as he gently pushed Vanelli's knife-wielding hand away.

Vanelli knew he would have to learn to fire a rifle, but he also knew that he had a valuable talent, namely a skill with the knife.

The company moved out and marched toward Virginia. They bivouacked that night in Maryland, and rumor had it that they would be marching down the Blue Ridge Mountains. Several days later, they heard gunfire near Winchester, Virginia.

"The captain wants to see ye, Vanelli," Sergeant Robbins said.

"What's he want?" Benjamin asked.

"Ye don't ask that, kid. Ye just go see him. Understand?"

"OK," he replied as he followed the sergeant to the Captain's tent.

"We are going to approach a Reb encampment tomorrow. I understand you are good with a knife, is that so?" the captain asked.

"Sure, I'm able to use a knife."

"You say 'sir' when you speak to the captain, Vanelli!" Robbins said.

"I want you to work with Sergeant Robbins and take out the sentries just before daybreak. We'll then go in and surprise the camp. Do you understand?"

"I understand, sir." Vanelli felt the pride in being given an important assignment.

"There's one. See him?" the Sergeant whispered.

Ben nodded, though it was probably too dark for Sergeant Robbins to see his chin. He then stood and silently crept up to the sentry. He held the knife ready to cut the sentry's throat. He hesitated about five feet from the sentry, partially hidden behind a tree. *He's just a kid. I can't just cut his throat,* he mused. *If he were attacking me, I could cut him from crotch to gullet, but I can't just silently kill him for nothing.*

Ben turned and silently made his way back to the sergeant.

"What's the matter? Scared of doing it?" Sergeant Robbins asked in a whisper.

"Not scared. Just don't like to slice somebody up like a sneak," Ben responded.

Robbins sneaked up to the sentry and dispatched him quickly. He then sent Vanelli back to the company.

Following the skirmish, Benjamin was again summoned by the captain. "Vanelli, you can't shoot, you won't kill the sentries with a knife. What the hell are you good for?" the captain asked.

"I ain't afraid. I'll fight alongside anyone. I just can't kill a man not even looking at me."

"Well, I have one more task that needs doing, and I'm going to let you give it a try. It is pretty obvious that you are quick on your feet, so maybe this will work. Do you know what black powder is?"

"Sure. It's what we use in our guns."

"See that keg? That's black powder or gun powder." The captain pointed to what looked like a small barrel. They were gathered in the captain's tent, and he had a table set up with maps on it.

"I see it," Ben replied.

"You make a trail of gun powder leading up to the keg, and then light the end of the trail and run like hell. When the line of powder burns to the keg, it explodes. Can you follow what I'm saying?"

"Yup. The fire runs along that trail of powder and causes the powder in the keg to explode."

"I want you to blow up a bridge. I have to tell you, the last person we had doing this didn't use a long enough trail, and he blew himself up. You can't use too long a trail, or it might be discovered by the Rebs, and they'd put it out. OK?" The captain was watching his reaction.

"Sounds easy enough to me," Vanelli said.

"Why do we have to do all of these things in the dark?" Vanelli mused, though he knew the answer. He was crawling toward a bridge that was outlined against the lighter sky. It was raining slightly, and he was sweating. He carried a sack full of powder on his right shoulder and the keg of powder under his left arm. Sarge had explained where the explosive was to be placed and had even drawn a rough picture of the bridge. *At least I don't have to go into the water. Might as well, however*, he mused. *I'm already so wet. Wonder if the water affects the powder?* It took nearly half an hour to place the powder where he had been told and to string the trail of powder to a safe distance. Then came the tricky part. He had to light the powder trail, and run like hell. He was sure that when he lit the powder, if there were Rebs near, he'd be shot. Still, that was why he had worked his way here. In fact, he had been told that the Rebs would not be along until nearly noon. Blowing up the bridge was to stop them before they could cross this river.

He fetched the matches from his pocket and scraped off the wax which had been used to keep them dry. He then struck the match to his belt buckle and dropped it on the end of the powder line. The powder began sputtering. Once he was certain that it was lit, he turned and ran back toward camp. He had traveled about two hundred yards when the keg exploded. He dropped to the ground and looked back. A portion of the bridge was gone and there was a lot of smoke and dust where it had been. He felt a sense of pride of accomplishment in that he was responsible for striking a blow against the rebels.

The next day, they moved further south, and he was given another bridge to destroy. Then came an opportunity to place a charge where it could destroy a big gun of the rebels. He had been given a horse with an old beat-up McClelland saddle and had been promoted to corporal. With three men to protect his flanks, he rode into a pass in the mountains. He thought they were in West Virginia, but perhaps it was the western slopes of the Virginia Mountains.

He set the charges and moved back to the edge of the pass. He had the cigar going pretty well but had a long powder trail, so he was worried that the Rebs would be able to spot the fire and cut the line of powder before it blew. He heard them coming for quite some time before they began to roll their big cannon into the pass. He lit the fuse, mounted up, and rode like fury away from the inevitable explosion.

The four men made it back to camp, and soon Sarge rode in. He had been positioned where he could watch the action from across the hillside. He clapped Benjamin on the back and with a grin, told the captain that at least four cannons were out of commission.

The unit was joined with another larger unit, forming a regiment. Two days later, they encountered a large enemy force. For eight hours, there was fierce fighting. Black smoke hung over the entire area. They often could not see beyond the ends of their own rifles.

When the firing ceased, they knew they had won the battle, but there was no satisfaction, merely exhaustion.

"Vanelli!" called the sergeant. "Take a dozen men, and go out and fetch the dead."

"You trying to get me killed, Sarge?" he asked.

"There's a truce flag for both sides to gather their dead. Get on out there."

Vanelli picked the men and began to gather bodies. It was the most gruesome task he had ever had to do. The stench of battle—smoke, death, and fear—assailed their nostrils. What a horrible way to live or to die, he thought.

They had nearly a hundred prisoners to guard that night, and then a squad of men was detached to march the prisoners to a train where they would be transported to a prison. The unit pulled back into Pennsylvania. They bivouacked for three days to rest up from the battle and to await replacements, before again moving on.

During the rest, Lieutenant Anders came to Vanelli and said that he needed his horse to ride to another regiment.

Ben hated to let his horse go, but the lieutenant merely took him. Two days, later the lieutenant was back, but no horse. Lieutenant Anders was standing in front of his tent when Vanelli's anger boiled over. "Lieutenant, where's my horse?" he demanded.

I left him where I found him," Anders replied.

"He ain't there and I don't believe you left him there."

"Watch how you talk, corporal!" the lieutenant said with some menace.

"You're a damn horse thief," Vanelli exploded.

"I'll have you court martialed for that, corporal," said Anders.

Vanelli then drove his fist into the lieutenant's stomach and flattened him with a haymaker.

As a result of these actions, Vanelli was court marshaled and stripped of his rank. Back to being Private Vanelli, and being restricted to his tent when not in action, Ben was still fuming about the loss of the horse and saddle.

Vanelli spent several days idling about camp. They did little training and no combat. Then one morning, the order came to strike camp. The troops marched through the city of Philadelphia. A few people lined the streets and clapped their hands and waved. It was not a large crowd and not very boisterous.

The regiment had no idea where they were going until they arrived at the docks. A ship was waiting there, and they all boarded. It was crowded, not only with several hundred men but several horses and a large load of supplies—ammunition, canned food, flour, and other material.

Finding a few square feet to bed down, the men, tired from the long march, were soon asleep. Sometime during the night, the ship slipped its mooring and sailed down the river into the Chesapeake Bay. For several days, they rose, lined up for meals, and sat around the ship, sometimes cleaning and polishing their weapons. Often a card game was going in one part of the ship or another, and then they lined up for another meal and slept. Rumors were rampant as to where they were going, but no one could confirm anything.

One rumor was that they were going to land in Mobile, another Savanah. A non commissioned officer with a Maine accent insisted that they would be landing in New Orleans, while another insisted they would sail up the Mississippi River to flank the Rebs on the west. When they landed, no one knew where they were for several days, until they found they had landed in Georgia.

Unloading the ship took three days of hard labor, for they had to carry much of the load by wading in shallow water from the ship to the shore. This could only be done during low tide so was often done during the hours of darkness. It was hard to tell whether schlepping goods from the ship or standing guard was worse. While the ship off-loading was hard work, there was always a cool breeze on the water. Mosquitoes, on the other hand, ate a standing sentry almost to death. They soon found that the reason for so many mosquitoes was that they were camped on the edge of a large swamp.

Once the ship was off-loaded, it sailed at the next high tide and the men felt abandoned.

"Vanelli, the captain wants you," shouted Sergeant Robbins.

"OK, Sarge," Vanelli responded.

"You wanted me, Captain?"

"Yes, Vanelli. I need a runner."

"I'm here," Vanelli, responded with enthusiasm. He was tired of mosquitoes and working on the camp.

"Vanelli, there's a Union company camped about twenty miles north of us. Look at this map. See that road, sometimes not more than a pathway, but it is the safest route to that company. I want you to take two men and carry a message to Captain Early, commander of that company and bring back our orders. I'm counting on you doing that in two days. If we don't hear from you by midnight day after tomorrow, I'll assume you were captured and we'll strike out on our own. I really want to have us strike at the same time as that company so let's get there and back. You got it?"

"I got it Cap'n!"

"One more thing. Look again at this map. There're Rebs all around but there are definitely forces camped here and here. Move through that area with extreme caution."

"Will do, Cap'n. I'm always cautious."

Sergeant Robbins handed him a small package of food and reminded him to fill his canteen before starting out. Then he pulled out his pistol and handed it to Vanelli. "That rifle is too big and awkward for you to take when you'll be running a good bit of the time. Just be sure to bring it back."

"Thanks, Sarge." Vanelli was taken aback by the sarge's generosity.

Vanelli selected two men: a red headed fellow named Dod McDuffy who, like Vanelli, was from Brooklyn and a lanky boy who rarely spoke named George Dodge, who hailed from Maine. They headed north almost immediately. They followed the well-marked pathway but were always watching for other people. They moved rapidly for several hours without sighting any one.

They came to a shallow stream, which worried them, since they would no longer be screened by trees and would be in the open for some time. After carefully moving up and down the stream a short ways, they decided that it would be safe to cross. Vanelli sent McDuffy across first and had him set up surveillance on the other side. Both McDuffy and Dodge had rifles, so after McDuffy made it safely across, Vanelli made the dash, leaving Dodge to watch the south side of the river.

Both men were then carefully camouflaged, and it was Dodge's turn. He didn't move. Vanelli watched and waited for him to start, but he remained in the brush where Vanelli had left him. "What the hell is the matter with him? Why doesn't he get over here?" McDuffy whispered.

Vanelli put his finger to his lips so that McDuffy would not speak again and continued to watch for Dodge. Suddenly there was a shot and thrashing about where Dodge had been. Then two men moved cautiously out of the woods and peered across the river. As much as he hated to do so, Vanelli reluctantly signaled McDuffy to move on. The mission was more important than trying to capture or kill two Rebs who might only be the scouts for a larger group.

As they progressed, they passed fields and farms by circling around them. They avoided outbuildings and remained in the trees or underbrush. Most of these places appeared to be abandoned. Once they saw a young white woman and a black man working, side by side, in what appeared to be a kitchen garden.

Though they had attempted to hurry, the additional time taken to be cautious resulted in their reaching the union encampment about dusk. There was a brief holdup as they approached the sentry for the encampment, as the sentry was reluctant to let them pass with their weapons. A signal to the commander resolved the problem.

After delivering his message, Vanelli and McDuffy found a meal and a place to sleep. Wakened at daybreak, the two runners begged a cup of weak coffee and, getting their reply, left to return to their unit. As they were making their way back, McDuffy said, "What if you're captured or shot and that message gets into Johnny Reb's hands? That would be pretty bad, wouldn't it?"

"That's true. Maybe we should both memorize what it says and destroy the copy. Then if one of us gets shot the other can perhaps get through with the message."

"Good idea!" McDuffy agreed. So they stopped for a few minutes and tore open the message and read it. They both felt that they could remember what it said, so they carefully tore up the written message and buried the scraps of paper. Again, they started traveling.

While skirting one of the plantations, they noticed that there was considerable activity there. At least four horses were being held by four men, and another dozen or so men were resting under the large trees in the yard. All of the men were in the gray uniform of the Confederacy. While the men were obviously resting, some were eating, and others were merely lying down. There was no evidence of the officers who would have been riding the horses.

"Bet those horses belong to officers who are in the house." McDuffy said.

"I know. I wonder if that is the entire unit, or if these are merely the forward guard." Vanelli mused. "We can't stop and waste time here. We have to get this message back to the regiment. Too bad, though. It might be useful to know what's going on here."

Soon they reached the stream that they had crossed on the way north. Again, Vanelli sent McDuffy across first. Once he made it, Vanelli made his dash. As he splashed up the far bank, he heard a cry from the north side. A number of Rebs were racing toward the river. Vanelli raced to the brush and quietly urged McDuffy to run, which he did.

Screening himself as best he could, he waited for the Rebs to enter the stream. Soon he was rewarded with two of them splashing into the water. There were a total of four, so two remained behind to protect those who led. When they were approximately halfway across, Vanelli decided to try out Sarge's pistol. Never having been much of a shot, he was not expecting to do much more than slow them down. His first shot hit the water in front of the lead man. His second shot his the second man in the shoulder, causing him to fall into the water. Then the two Rebs on the other bank each fired, kicking up dirt near Vanelli. Knowing that he had only six shots, Vanelli waited to see what the lead man would do. Meanwhile, the Rebs on the bank were reloading their single-shot rifles.

It occurred to Vanelli that they may not have known that there were two men. Perhaps if he surrendered, he could delay their searching for McDuffy, who could then get the message back to Regiment. But he couldn't make himself quit. He wasn't a quitter. Following their next volley, he again fired as fast as he could squeeze the trigger. When he ran out of bullets, he rose and raced away toward the regiment. He had not traveled more than a hundred yards when he tripped and fell. Two Rebs who had crossed the river below where he had guarded it immediately fell upon him. He was now their prisoner.

There were approximately twenty prisoners and twice that number of guards. The guards, however, were not well-disciplined soldiers. Some of them were just plain mean, prodding the prisoners with rifles and using any excuse to batter them. Others were merely sloppy and careless. The union soldiers were not much more disciplined, but Ben and a Pennsylvanian named Alex found an opportunity to whisper to each other and develop a half-baked plan to escape.

Having identified which guards were most careless, they watched for the chance to slip away when those were on guard. Though shackled, they had worked out a way to open the shackles, which had been slovenly attached and were old. Alex noticed that the weakest guard was on duty and pointed this out to Vanelli. All of the prisoners had been searched for weapons, but the search neglected to closely examine Vanelli's boots where he had hidden his knife. Toward the end of the guard change, when those on duty were most tired and least alert, the two men carefully removed their shackles and, using the knife, dispatched the nearest guard. Taking his rifle, they carefully slipped into the underbrush.

Hurrying as fast as they could without making a lot of noise, they managed to reach a stream and quickly splashed across. Just as they reached the far bank, a shot rang out from pursuers, and Alex collapsed into the water. Glancing back, Vanelli realized that there was nothing he could do for him, so he melted into the brush and kept traveling. For the next two days, he fought mosquitoes and hunger and dodged bands of rebels. He tried to keep headed north but sometimes had to skirt swamps, villages, or rebels.

Vanelli awoke shivering. Early spring in the Carolinas did not mean sleeping temperatures, and he was covered with dew. He had managed to work his way around a small village after dark. This was the third day since he had escaped from the group of prisoners, and he finally felt safe enough to sleep. He had crashed into a briar patch in the dark, and the moonlight showed him a small clearing, partially forested with pine trees. The pine needles made a comfortable enough bed that, combined with exhaustion, let him immediately fell asleep.

He arose from his slumber, shivering and damp, and peered about, trying to orient himself. He heard the gurgle of a stream nearby but could see no evidence of people, so he drank some water and splashed his face with the icy stream. He then began to move in what he thought was a northerly direction. He tried to conjure up a picture in his mind of where he might be. He had seen a good map before he had been sent on his trek to obtain information from Captain Early, but he wasn't sure how far he had been forced to go when he was a prisoner. When he had fled from the prisoners, he tried to keep his direction northerly but, at times, had to veer away to avoid towns and groups of Rebs.

If he had traveled as far as he thought he had, he should be somewhere in either North Carolina or Virginia. At some point, he should be striking the coastal area in southernmost Virginia.

His immediate problem, however, was hunger. He couldn't remember the last time he had eaten more than some raw vegetables stolen from a field or a handful of grain that he had grabbed in a cow barn. In both of these instances, he was fearful of being caught, because he was too near civilization. He had thought of catching a fish in one of the small streams that he had crossed but had no line or hook. He spent an hour attempting to stab one with a sharp stick but was unsuccessful.

It was late at night when he approached a farm and found a hen house. He carefully opened the pen door and began searching nests for eggs. In spite of his caution, he disturbed the chickens, and they began fluttering their wings and clucking. He found no eggs and was about to grab a chicken when he saw a light. A woman with a lantern and a shotgun shouted at him, "What do you think you're doing? Put your hands over your head, or I'll shoot."

Benjamin smiled at the lady and said, "I'm sorry to have offended ye ma'am. I'm terrible hungry and thought I might find an egg to eat. I'll just move along and not bother ye anymore."

He started to sidle out of the hen's pen, when she brought the shotgun up again and said, "Hold it right there, Yankee. Did you find any eggs?"

"No'm I sure didn't."

"Them damn hens stopped laying eggs."

Ben had no answer to that, never having had much to do with hens or any other livestock, so he kept quiet. She seemed to have something in mind other than shooting him, and he was willing to listen to any alternative to that.

"Do you know how to kill a chicken?" she asked.

Ben had no idea how to kill a chicken, but how hard could it be? If this was the alternative to being shot, he'd sure give it a try. "Sure, I can kill it."

"I've seen the men do it by chopping off her head and plucking the feathers, but I can't do it," she said.

That was good information and would make Ben seem as though he knew what he was doing.

"Do you have an axe?" he asked.

She lowered the shotgun and headed into a nearby shed, so he followed.

"Here's all I got!" She said waving her hand toward a shelf with a few rusty tools.

Ben found a rusty axe and turned around as she said, "Here's a block to chop her head off with." She had stepped back a ways and again acted like she knew how to use that shotgun.

Ben went back to the hen house with her trailing him with the shotgun. He tried several times before he finally managed to grab a chicken. Holding it by the body, he couldn't see how he could chop its head off but finally realized that he had to hold it by the legs. It flopped around a lot before he finally managed to hack its head off, and he became splattered with a lot of blood as the beast flopped and fluttered after the head was gone. If he had not been so hungry, he wasn't sure he could manage to eat this thing.

Finally, he pulled most of the feathers off and turned to the woman. She had stood well back from the activity and had relaxed the shotgun pose somewhat but still clung to the gun.

"What do you want me to do with this now?" Ben asked.

"Bring it into the kitchen and I'll boil some water. You should get some of that blood off you first. Here, give me the chicken, and you go out to that pump there."

After they ate the entire chicken, the woman began gathering up the dishes and heated some water to wash them. Ben watched and tried to decide what he would do. He wanted to be on his way, but his belly was full, and he was bone-tired. In fact, his head nodded a time or two, before she turned and said, "You can dry these. I guess you're not goin' to run off before you get some sleep."

Ben's decision was made. He'd get a night's sleep and maybe some breakfast before heading north again. He had no idea where he was or where he could find some Union troops.

When she finished with the dishes, she looked at him and said, "I don't know what to do about you. I should shoot you or turn you over to the army, but I don't know when any of them will come by here again. I guess I'll just let you go when you want. You aren't goin' to burn my farm, are you?"

"Course not! You can keep that shotgun close, and I'll just sleep here on the couch. If you want, I'll chop up a little more wood and kill you another chicken before I go. I don't like killin' and shootin', but I sure don't want to spend any more time as a prisoner of them Johnny Rebs. They were some mean fellers."

"You can sleep in the barn. There's some hay there, and, come morning, you better git. I don't trust you, but you seem like a nice enough feller, so I'm not going to shoot you if you get out of here."

Ben awoke as the sun was coming up. There was some frost on the ground, but he had slept well and was ready to head out. As far as possible, he stayed on northbound paths and roads. Whenever he heard voices or horses, he was alert to duck into the brush. Now and then, he found it necessary to leave the paths and make his way through field and forests.

He found an abandoned farm and crawled into a pile of musty hay for part of the first night out. He awoke to voices and the rattle of horse hooves. Lying as still as possible, he listened to the voices and caught enough of the conversation to realize that it was a small band of Rebels foraging for food. As soon as they left, he peered out and saw that they had headed west. He was shivering from the cold so decided that movement was the best way to get warm. He found enough moonlight to see the road and headed north again.

He crossed streams and crashed through briars but kept going. When it became too dark to travel, he tried to hide in the brush and sleep but was both hungry and uncomfortable. Still he kept moving.

Suddenly his nose detected the odor of cow manure, and his mouth watered for some fresh milk. He tried to search out the source of that odor and soon discovered a field with a barn and house on the other side of it. There was no way he could cross that open field without being seen unless he waited until dark. He hated to waste a full day's travel, so, with great reluctance and hope for future discoveries, he proceeded north.

He found a grove of oaks and eked a few morsels of nut meat out of a handful of acorns. Hearing the jangle of trace chains from a team of horses, he crept to the edge of a road and watched a wagon go past, driven by a black man and pulled by a team of draft horses. When the wagon was out of sight, he darted across the road and again melted into the brush.

Coming to a large river, he sat down and began to despair. How could he ever cross that? He could swim a little, but the stream was swift and wide. There was no way he could ever make it across swimming. Hungry, tired, and discouraged, he was tempted to give up. He remembered how badly the guards had treated the prisoners, and he couldn't imagine becoming a prisoner again.

As he sat, despondent and hungry, he had an idea. If it were dark, he could probably cross a bridge. He had several hours of daylight to find that bridge, and then could wait until dark to sneak across. As a soldier, he had blown up enough bridges that he knew how important they were to the army. If he found one, it might be guarded, but it was his only chance.

Keeping the river in sight, he traveled upstream. It was nearly two hours before he spotted a bridge. Sure enough, there were guards. Benjamin found a knoll where he could remain hidden yet peer through the brush to watch the guards.

Two guards took turns walking across the bridge and back. While one crossed the bridge, the other sat on a stump near the end of the bridge or lolled about. They didn't seem to have any particular pattern to their schedule. They might cross every fifteen minutes or so, or they might both sit and chat for an hour before one of them crossed the bridge.

He was concentrating so hard on watching the guards that he almost missed a wagon being pulled by a team of horses that drove up to the bridge. The guards seemed to know the driver, who stopped and talked with them for a minute, and then drove across. A while later, a carriage came the other way. The traffic gave Benjamin an idea. He hoped a loaded wagon might come along, and he could slip into the load and cross undetected.

The sun was nearly gone when exactly what he hoped for happened. Both guards were at the end of the bridge when Benjamin spotted a wagon loaded with barrels coming along the road. Moving quickly, he was ready before the wagon made it around the curve to approach the bridge. He slipped out onto the road and carefully climbed onto the wagon. He had to push a barrel aside slightly to make room to squeeze between them, and the driver looked back to see if a barrel had tipped over, but he did not see Benjamin.

At the bridge, one of the guards called out, "What ye' got in them barrels, Andy? Ain't whiskey by any chance, is it?"

"Sorry boys, these're empty. Maybe I can fetch some liquor when I come back t'morra," the driver replied but didn't stop the wagon. Benjamin crouched among the barrels and prayed they couldn't see him. He wished the horses moved faster. It seemed to take forever for them to cross the bridge.

After reaching the other side, Benjamin remained crouched down as the wagon slowly made its way through a village and turned into a side street. *Oh, my God,* Ben thought. *He's going to stop in the village and unload. What can I do?*

The wagon stopped, and the driver began yelling at the horses to back up to a large building of some sort. *Maybe a warehouse where he'll unload the barrels,* Ben thought. As he readied himself to run, he waited for the driver to come to the back of the wagon. Instead, Benjamin heard the jangle of traces and the driver cursing the horses. Then he heard the horses moving away with the man driving them. They were unhitched from the wagon. Benjamin peered out and found that everything was deserted. He made his way cautiously out of the wagon, keeping in the shadows, for it was nearly dark now. He sneaked out of the town.

He skirted around several small bands of foragers and wondered why they were foraging and in such small bands. Where was the army?

He came upon a large body of water and decided it must be the ocean. He had to move back further west, or he would be traveling in the open. He wasn't familiar with the country and didn't know whether the water he saw was ocean or the Chesapeake Bay. It didn't matter all that much though. He needed to keep going north if he was going to find Union troops.

Two miserable days later, early in the evening, he was skirting a town when he heard music and dancing. This seemed strange, so he tried to sneak in closer to find out what was going on. He saw a crowd of people singing and carrying on. None of them were in uniform, so he couldn't tell if they were northerners or southerners.

He was trying to stay out of sight when someone behind him said, "Come on. Join the celebration."

Ben turned and saw a young lad about sixteen. "What celebration?" he asked.

"The war is over."

"Who won?" Ben asked.

"You don't see any gray uniforms there do you?" laughed the young lad.

It took little urging for Ben to join the group marching and singing. However, he soon found that not everyone was happy with the outcome. Several people were standing on the street, dejected and silent. However, Ben was finally glad to come in out of the woods.

The Survivors

The noise, the stench, the heat and cold,
Things remembered with fear so old.
It's become a part of life we live
And so affects all we can give.

The guns may cease, the bombs as well
The sounds live on in mind and soul
The fear is there, a living thing
Fear of guilt, not fear of dying.

I stand guilty; fear has not left,
I mourn those heroes of fear bereft.
Yet would I change with them today?
Guilty, fear-laden, I dare not say.

Robin Hoodwink

———◆———

SHE STOPPED THE TRACTOR AT the top of the knoll and gazed back across the field. The pattern of bronze windrows of hay gave her pleasure. This was what made farming so satisfying. Golden sun glistening on the intricate design left by the rake was all the artistry Glenda needed. She heard the chunk-a-chunk of the baler in the southern field and knew that she would soon need to bring the truck to load the bales.

Old Farnsworth would be ready to load, and Eddie would have that field baled in short order. Seemed like as beautiful as the results of your work, there just wasn't enough time to appreciate and enjoy it. She didn't mind farming. At times like this one, she even found pleasure in it. Yet she longed for something, for the sound of surf gently lapping at the beach, the warm sun penetrating sore muscles, the fragrance of tropical flowers that she remembered from the honeymoon that had taken all their savings.

"Chunk-a-chunk." The sound of the baler brought her out of her reverie. She put the tractor in gear and drove into the yard. Farnsworth yelled at her, "Get hitched to the hay wagon; got a storm comin'."

Pulling the pin from the power takeoff, she soon had the wagon hooked to the tractor and followed Farnsworth to the south field. Eddie would have the north field baled shortly and would be along to help, but, meanwhile, she and Farnsworth loaded the truck and took a load to the barn. Rushing back to the field, they quickly filled the two vehicles and met Eddie at the barn to unload.

The air was heavy with humidity, and sweat poured off them all. A swallow of water tossed off in a dash, and they were back in the vehicles, headed for the northern field. Both rigs were loaded with bales when the first raindrops began to pelt them. A dozen bales were left, but those loaded made it to the barn before the wind whipped the rain with a frenzy.

Glancing out of the door into the torrential downpour, they were amazed at the violence of the wind. When they had unloaded the hay, they tramped down the steps from the loft to the stable and proceeded to the milk room. The milking machines were rigged, and the first four cows were let into the milking parlor when the power went off. Lightning and thunder boomers had been rattling about, but to lose power at this time was a bit more than inconvenient.

It took nearly a half hour for Farnsworth to tinker with the gasoline-powered generator before he had it operating. It provided enough power to run the machines and extract the milk from the forty-two milkers. Another half hour cleaning up, and they could go in for supper. The rain had let up, and the wind ceased.

Glenda and Eddie sloshed through rivulets of water on the way to their double-wide set up about a quarter mile from the main house. Farnsworth had long before pushed his way through the mud and settled into his kitchen chair to watch the news before remembering that there was no power for the television. Glenda and Eddie saw the flickering of a candle as they passed his kitchen window. They soon had their candles lit and found cold meat and milk for dinner.

Morning comes very early on the farm, and Glenda and Eddie were up before the sun. They fired up the generator and milked, but they yearned for a cup of hot coffee. Still no power.

Farnsworth stumbled out and drove off with the truck. Soon he tore back into the yard. "There's a hell of a big tree across the road, right by the gateway to the north field," he said. "Better get the chainsaw, and see if we can cut it up."

Glenda and Eddie put the chainsaw in the back of the truck, found some gasoline-oil mix and the sharpener, and Farnsworth drove them down to the tree. It was an enormous pine that had been uprooted. Apparently the wind had tipped it over, roots and all.

"What do you suppose that is?" Glenda pointed at something that looked like fabric with roots twined around it. The root structure was seven or eight feet across, and it was a stretch to reach this piece of whatever.

Eddie got a stick and poked at it, trying to pry it loose.

Farnsworth stepped around to where he could see, and he pulled at the roots. "Looks like an old suitcase," he said. "Don't know what it would be doin' there. Somebody musta left it by that old tree, and the roots growed around it."

"They'd a had to bury it for it to be in them roots like that," Eddie said as he jabbed the stick again.

Just then, the rotting leather of the old case gave way, and money began falling out. "My Lord, look at that!" Farnsworth exclaimed.

Eddie renewed his efforts with vigor, and soon the ground was littered with green paper. Glenda and Farnsworth picked them up as fast as they could. There were hundred-dollar bills, fifties, twenties, and a few tens. Thousands and thousands of dollars. Some still retained a band holding them together. Eddie took off his shirt and used it to hold the money while they gathered it up and headed for the house.

"Where do you suppose this all came from?" Glenda asked.

"You know," Farnsworth said, "I'll betcha this was that bank-robbery money."

"What bank-robbery money?" Eddie asked.

Farnsworth leaned back and related quite a tale.

"Seems like it was in '34 or '35," he began. "There were these two brothers, the Hadley brothers, Rap and Skip, just terrorizing the area. They had robbed banks in the eastern part of the state and seemed to be working this way. Sure enough, one day, they held up the local bank and made off with everything in it. Wasn't much money around in those days, but, for some reason, that bank had quite a lot of ready cash. Those scoundrels got it all.

"Now the sheriff took out after them, and they ran along some back roads, until they got a flat tire. Their old Studebaker, stolen car it was, blew a tire right near this farm. I was pretty young then, but I remember goin' up and lookin' at that car with my dad. There were sheriff deputies, state police, and game wardens all chasing those boys.

"Along about dark, they caught up with them. Had them backed up against the river, and neither one of them could swim. There was some shooting, and Rap Hadley—his real name was Ralph—was badly wounded. Died before they could get him to a hospital. His brother wasn't even nicked.

"The sheriff had some tough time keeping the boys from beating up Skip, because he wouldn't tell anyone where he hid the money. I'll tell you there was more diggin' and searchin' in those woods than anyone could imagine. Everybody in the county had a look at least once, tryin' to find that loot. And everyone was lookin' near where they caught them two. Nobody ever figured that they would have stashed it so near the car."

"So nobody knows that this money is here? What about the other Hadley brother, Skip?" Glenda asked.

"He died in jail," Farnsworth said. "Never told anyone where he'd hid the loot, far's we can tell. He's been gone thirty years or more. Died in his sleep, they say. Nobody knows about this money 'cept us."

"It must belong to the bank or to the people who lost it when the bank was robbed," Eddie said in a regretful tone.

"Well, the insurance company or the government or some-body settled up something on it. I don't recall, exactly, but I know that everybody who had money there got some of it back," Farnsworth said.

Glenda thought for a minute, and then said, "It belongs to the bank or to whomever the bank was insured by." Then with some conviction and firmness, she said, "We need to take it in."

"Hold on now," Farnsworth said, "I don't hold with stealing, but we don't know for sure that this is the robbery money, and it was found on my property." He was thinking of a new tractor, maybe with air conditioning, and perhaps fixing up the barn. Maybe even one of those big blue "Harvestore" silos.

"I don't know," Eddie said, "I kind of agree with Glenda. This ain't our money, much as I'd like to have some of it." He was thinking how great it could have been to have one of those new four-by-four extended-cab GMC 1500s, but Glenda made sense.

Glenda was adamant. "That money isn't ours. It belongs to the bank. I don't think I could walk down the street and face the people of this town if we didn't return it."

Farnsworth wouldn't let go, however. "Look, now. We've counted this out, and it comes to $586,120. If we split that down the middle, we'd each get $293,060, almost three hundred grand apiece. I'd be willing to do that, even though it was found on my farm."

"I was thinking more like three ways," Eddie said. "$195,373 each, and you could have the extra dollar. Seems like there were three of us found that—or, actually, it was Glenda that found it."

"Never mind how we would divide that up. It doesn't belong to us," Glenda's voice was getting stronger. "Mr. Farnsworth, do you have a suitcase that we can put this into while we take it back?"

Reluctantly, Farnsworth went into his bedroom and returned with a beat-up Gladstone with one strap broken. "Here's a case, but we shouldn't be too hasty with this. Why don't we sleep on it tonight and make the decision in the morning? Can't get out right now with that tree in the way anyhow."

"OK, we can wait until tomorrow, but it's got to go back," Glenda stated.

"I'll just put it in my closet, and we'll talk about it in the morning'," Farnsworth said.

"No, I'll put it in our trailer and make sure that it goes back in the morning," Glenda said as she hefted the heavy bag and stared defiantly at the two men.

No more was said about the money as they cut up the fallen pine and did evening chores. Glenda had taken the suitcase and slid it under their bed.

Farnsworth slept fitfully all night and was up in time to help with the chores. He went to the barn and found that he was the first there, so he started the generator and began milking. It wasn't like Glenda and Eddie to be late. In fact, he had not known them to fail to show up for morning milking in the two years they had worked for him. When he finished chores, he decided to see what had happened, so he strolled down to their double-wide. The truck was gone, and no one answered the door.

"They couldn't have gone to the bank this early! Where the devil are they?" he muttered to himself.

A week later, he got a package in the mail. He opened it up and found that it was a battered Gladstone with one strap repaired. He looked again at the mailing paper and finally made out the postmark, "Jamaica."

The Shires of Berk

———

Valleys of streams and hills where trees stand;
The mill folk and those who work the land;
And history so deep in blood, joy, and work
Lies the land that I love, the Shires of Berk.

Snow-shrouded hills in winter so grand;
Deep loam valleys to make the land
Where farmers grow crops to feed all folk,
Till a flood or storm, nature's cruel joke.

Glorious blooms in spring burst forth
Earth's natural cycle shows the worth
Of summer's bounteous pleasures
A time for laying away land's treasures.

When the hills are painted with fall's tint
And winter's portent is felt with that hint
We fear not the snows; this is the reason;
In this land, each is a wondrous season.

Year- 'round we find in this beauteous place
There exists in the land of God given grace
A harmony felt among all living things,
The wonder of life each season brings.

It Always Rains for a Funeral

Governor Saltonstall turned a valve, which opened the Norumbega Reservoir to a flow of water from Quabbin on October 23, 1940. He remarked, "This is the greatest engineering work ever undertaken in this part of the country. It means that fresh water now completes an underground journey to greater Boston from sixty miles out in the heart of Massachusetts."

IT ALWAYS RAINS FOR A funeral. Of course, this is not a funeral. The funeral was almost a year ago. No, actually, the funeral was nearly ten years ago. He was buried in booze, not in dirt.

The rain is soaking into my shoes. The fragrance of the rain, earth, and wet grass was vaguely familiar and reminiscent of my childhood, back when we lived on the farm that was now gone.

Mother would call out for us to get in out of the rain. The rain didn't hurt us, and it was desperately needed for the crops. We, my friend Bobby and I, splashed through the puddles in our bare feet and chased after the cows. Perhaps we followed the plow as the horses pulled while Dad steered, picking up worms and night crawlers to use as bait for fishing in the river. We didn't have much, but we lived a full and happy life. We did well enough that I got into college and even got a commission when the war started.

I wonder about Bobby. When he got sacked on the football field in his junior year, it pretty well changed our lives. His injury prevented his joining the army, so we sort of lost track of each other. I probably should look him up, but maybe I'll wait until another time. This rain is coming down harder.

I guess I should go. No point in standing by this grave and totally ruining a good uniform at this late date. Never did get a chance to show off this uniform when he was alive. What a tragedy that such a kind and gentle man should become booze-soaked and die in a lonely life.

He might have still been alive if he had realized that I had survived and would be returning home.

My mind carried me back to that awful day. "We're not going to make it," were unnecessary words from the pilot, Bill O'Day. Not a single crew member had the least doubt that we were going into the drink. O'Day had nursed the big B-24 on one engine as far as he could. At least we had a chance that the Brits' rescue boats could reach us.

We had been losing altitude since the German Fokker blasted our left engine before our escort fighters nailed him. The escort had nursed us along for a long way, but its fuel was getting low.

The channel was below us and getting nearer by the minute. Arthur Goins, the tail gunner was wounded, and the bombardier had been shot up so badly that we knew he was gone. I was unscathed as was Bill, and we were doing our best to maintain altitude and direction. It was decided that our best chance of survival was to ride the plane down rather than bail out.

"Arthur, are you OK?" Bill queried.

"My leg is bleeding, and I think it's broken, Cap, but I'll make it down," he replied.

"Nelson, what about you?" Bill asked the waist gunner.

"I'm OK, Cap." Nelson Walker was the youngest member of the crew and sounded as frightened as the rest of us felt.

"OK, everybody. Brace yourselves, and be ready to exit. I'll set it down as softly as possible, but it will be a hell of a jolt. Remember the drill, and get the hell out as quickly as possible."

The water was frigid. Bill didn't make it. I found Arthur floating in his Mae West but unconscious. I couldn't see Nelson, but I tied Arthur to my belt and searched for him. It was the longest day I had ever spent, but I was ecstatic when I spotted a vessel approaching us. Our orange vests helped the crew locate us, and we couldn't have been happier when they called out in French instead of German.

After pulling Arthur and me aboard, we saw that they had also found Nelson. We were all in bad shape from hypothermia and exhaustion. Our trials were not over yet, as the vessel was ostensibly a fishing boat and was bound to be questioned by the Germans when it reached land. After giving us hot soup and some dry clothes, they put us ashore on a small spit of land with directions inland. We bandaged Arthur's leg as best we could, and Nelson and I half carried him. He was in excruciating pain, and we had no morphine to help ease it. As we made our way along a weed-infested trail, we soon realized that we were totally lost. Having to stop and rest every a few minutes, darkness had overtaken us. We had run out of water and were totally exhausted, so we collapsed and attempted to keep each other warm.

When the sun started to peek through the surrounding foliage, we heard something crashing through the brush and weeds. They were going to pass us by, but then we heard French voices. I called out, though with some trepidation, I admit. It turned out to be search party looking for us. We were soon safely stashed in the cellar of a nearby farmhouse and given food, water, and warm clothes.

While Nelson and I could be sent out through the underground to return to England, Arthur would have to be turned over to the Germans, for he desperately needed medical care in a hospital. Though he was opposed to the idea of becoming a prisoner of war, he realized that with his raging fever and bouts of being comatose, he had no choice. It was either surrender or die.

Nelson and I were passed along in the depth of night from place to place until we reached Portugal. Finally, a ship was sailing to Ireland, and we eventually made our way back to England. It had taken three months to reach England from when we were picked up. For more than two of those months, we were officially listed as missing and presumed dead.

It was the "presumed dead" that was more than my dad could bear.

"Hello Tom!"

Startled out of my reverie, I turned to see who had come into the cemetery on such a lousy day in May. The rain was still pelting down, and the figure addressing me was wrapped in a poncho, so it was a moment before I recognized Robert. "How did you find me?" I asked.

"Saw a car and wondered who was dumb enough to slosh around out here in this weather."

"But you recognized me from back there? It's been a few years!"

"Who else would be in uniform and standing staring at that grave? Your dad's been in the ground almost a year. Anyone around here who'd remember him wouldn't take the time to come out here on a nice day, say nothing about a late-spring downpour."

"I dunno. There's fresh flowers here. How did that happen?"

Bob didn't bother answering. It wasn't necessary, because I knew the answer.

"Why don't you come to the house and have some hot coffee to take the chill off—or maybe a drink. You're not due back right off are you?"

"I've got a little time to kill. Sure, I'll have a cup of coffee with you and—June, isn't it?"

"Yeah. June and I and also Tommy and Alex."

"I'll follow you home," I told him.

The winding New England road was muddy but just as I remembered it, until we turned into his street.

The bungalow was neat and well kept. Despite the rain, I could see that it looked cozy and nice. Nothing like I was accustomed to either before I went into the air corps or since. I didn't know whether Bob still worked with his dad or had gone into something else since the war began. I knew that he was classified 4-F because of his knee. The house indicated that he was making a good living.

June met us at the door with a baby on her hip. I vaguely remembered her from school, but she had to have been two or three years younger than Bob and I.

"This is Alex. He's almost seven months old," she said. "I remember watching you play football, Tom. Welcome home!"

"Where's Tommy?" Bobby asked as he walked into the next room, searching.

"I think he is in the garage tinkering on that old car with Grandpa."

I began to regret coming here. I didn't want to see Bob's father. I hoped that it was not he in the garage.

"Well, let them tinker a while. Tom is soaking wet, and we need a cup of hot coffee. Would you rather have something else to take the chill off, Tom?"

"Coffee would be fine. I've never had a taste for the hard stuff, particularly after seeing what it did to my dad."

Bob, never one to beat around the bush, hit the subject head on. "That was certainly strange, the way your dad seemed to change. We all admired him. Heck, we even loved him. He was such a gentle man. He always had time for kids—I guess for everybody."

"He was still a gentle man. He just couldn't get over losing the farm. He loved farming. He used to say to me, 'Smell that hay; that's perfume for the gods. How about the fragrance of that grain—those old bossies will love that.' I have seen him spend hours contemplating a field of corn, trying to decide whether it would be better to pick the ears or put them into the chopper with the stalks."

"He never seemed to have any problems with livestock or machinery," Bob commented.

"Dad never did have any problems. He had challenges. If he spoke to a cow, he spoke softly as to a friend. When he worked with horses, he always talked gently and stroked them. But mostly, he loved the land. After harrowing a plowed field, he would scoop up a double handful of earth, and smell it, and then let it drift out of his hands, just feeling it. That land was the best farmland in the county."

"Why didn't he buy a farm when you moved? There must have been some for sale; 1935 was a poor time, and people who had cash money could buy most anything."

It's odd that Bob and I had never talked about this before. I guess he was embarrassed for me, and I was probably too embarrassed to bring it up.

"It wasn't the same. He didn't love land, he loved *that* land. You know! He fought hard against those city fellows. He wasn't trying to get a better price—he was trying to save what had been in his family since the Indians. You remember how we heard the arguments, peering in the window of the old Grange Hall."

"My dad did OK."

"Your dad hated farming. He jumped at the chance to sell out and get out. I give him credit. He found that little store near Athol and he made a go of it. It suits him fine to spend most of the day chatting up the old ladies and shooting the breeze with the farmers. By the way, what are you doing now?"

"June's dad owned the Chevrolet garage, and I went into business with him. We now have the Oldsmobile franchise and hope to grab the Buick and Cadillac dealership when they start making cars again. It's a good living. June's dad is a great guy—he's out in the garage with Tommy right now, tinkering on an old car." Bob continued, "What are you going to do when you get out?"

"I'm on my way from England to the Pacific. The war isn't over yet. I've been flying B-24 bombers, and I expect that I'll do some more of that for a while. After that, I don't know. I have no ties here, so I'll wait and see what comes up."

Perhaps Bob didn't realize what information I was after, because he seemed so open about everything. I decided that it was time to stop dancing around the issue. I needed to know what happened. "Exactly how did my dad die?" I assumed that is was cirrhosis of the liver, but when I finally got word, there were no specifics."

"No one told you? I guess that it must have been quite a while before you learned of his death, you being missing, an all.

When your dad got word that you were missing in action, he went into deep depression. He was in the alcoholism ward at the hospital, but they moved him into acute care. Somehow, he got some clothes on and walked out. Everyone assumed he had gone for some liquor, but no one could find him. The hospital called me, and I searched but couldn't find him anywhere."

"What did you do?" I asked.

"Wasn't much I could do. I kept looking for him—asked at all the bars around, checked with the liquor stores, called anyone I could think of that he might have gone to see. Nothing! A few days later, someone found a body floating in the reservoir, and it was finally identified as your dad. We managed to piece together that he had somehow gotten down to Gate 4, probably hitchhiked, and just walked into the water."

"I'm not terribly surprised. That would have been very near where our farm was. He never gave it up. Thank you for the information, and thank you for what you did for him over the years."

"It wasn't much. He wouldn't let anyone do much for him. He became a recluse, as you must remember. If he had waited a few more days, he would have learned that you were no longer missing but had been rescued."

"I will always feel somewhat guilty about being the precipitating cause of his death, but the real cause occurred long ago. I can't help but resent those Boston politicians who stole our land for a drink of water."

Thoughts on Veterans Day

They leave home with excitement in their breast,
beating.
A journey into adulthood of grand adventure
dreaming.
A band of brothers soon they will be
Standing proud and tall, fearless and free.
With a grin, gung-ho, a slap on the back,
Buddies for life; they charge into combat.
They kill, and on the adrenaline edge, they're alive,
And mourn those who yet did not survive.
Hard-eyed, tight-jawed, they return old men,
And in their dreams fight the battles again.
The wives, sweethearts, family, and friends who
remain
At home they also serve who stand and wait; their
love sustains.
The placard-waving crowd shares, too, in freedom's
light,

For those who serve the flag know what they do is
right.
And those who learn war but love peace
Ask that for their ultimate sacrifice
Not that God be on their side;
But that they be on God's.

The Lottery Ticket

I KNEW THAT IT WOULD be bad, but "bad" wasn't the word for it. It was horrible! Mom burst into tears and repeated over and over, "Oh my baby. I'm so ashamed!"

Dad, on the other hand, raved and ranted and became so red in the face that I thought he might have a heart attack. Eventually, they both became very angry, shouting, "We don't want you living here. Get out, and stay out!"

Tears blurred my vision as I made my way out the door and collapsed on the step. The next thing I knew, a bunch of my clothes landed on top of me. As the door slammed, I could not help sobbing more. "What can I do? Where can I go?"

I controlled my tears, picked up the clothes I could carry, and began walking. Eddie was twenty-one, had a job at the Chevrolet garage, and had his own apartment about a mile away. It took more than half an hour to walk to his place. I rang the bell and waited for him to open the door.

"What the hell are you doing here?" was his greeting.

More tears, and then the explanation that my folks had thrown me out. "Well, come on in then," he said. "You can stay here for now." I had been in his apartment before and remembered that neatness was not his strength. I pushed some dirty laundry off a chair and sat.

"You told them about the baby?" It was more of a statement than a question.

"I had to Eddie. I couldn't keep it a secret much longer."

"I told you that you should get an abortion. We can't afford no baby even if we did get married."

"I can't face an abortion, Eddie. Besides, I want to keep the baby. I thought you wanted to marry me."

"Marion, you can't get married without your folks' permission. You're only seventeen. Besides, I ain't ready to get married. We'll just live together for a while. But you need to get a job. I don't make enough money to support both of us."

I cleaned up the apartment and started looking for work. A convenience store two blocks away was looking for a counter person at minimum wage, so I started working there. Eddie finished off a six-pack of beer most evenings after work. When I got home, I would fix something to eat. For a while, everything was fine, but then Eddie began stopping at Smitty's, a local bar and grill, with some of his buddies and getting home later and later. I believed that this was because I was getting big and ugly with my belly like a watermelon. I didn't mind too much; I could come home and get my swollen feet up for a while.

Then, the baby arrived.

"Can't you keep that squallin' kid quiet!" Eddie was badly hungover on Sunday morning.

"I'll take him for a walk, Eddie. You can sleep."

"Fix me some eggs first. I got to get somethin' in my stomach."

"We don't have any eggs. You never gave me any money for groceries. I spent my last two dollars on milk for the baby."

"How come you spend all that money on the brat? I'm the one has to work and earn it." Eddie's face grew redder as he stomped about the apartment in his boxers. "Never mind fixing anything. I'll go down to Smitty's."

When he came home from work the next evening, he handed me a ten-dollar bill. I had not returned to work after the baby arrived, and the only money I had was what Eddie gave me. "Go down to your store and bring me back a six-pack, some cigarettes, and two lottery tickets. The rest of the money, you can spend on food for the brat."

Eddie had been drinking heavily when I returned and handed him his purchases. "Look at those lottery tickets, they have all the numbers together—sixteen, seventeen, nineteen, twenty. Why the hell did you do that?"

"The machine picked the numbers, Eddie. That's the way they came out."

"Stupid bitch! You shoulda asked for another ticket."

"I didn't have any more money, Eddie!"

His hand caught me across the face, and I fell back against the table. "Don't give me that sass. I gave you money, and you spent it on the brat." He raised his hand again, but I stepped back, and he dropped it. He threw the lottery tickets on the table and staggered into bed.

"Where're those lottery tickets?" Eddie demanded when he came home from work the next evening. "What did you do with them?"

"I gave them to you Eddie. Don't you remember? I handed them to you last night when I came back from the store."

He began tearing everything apart, trying to find the tickets. "What did you do with them? I remember that several of the numbers were in a line, and that's what I heard the winning ticket had. I want those tickets now." He grabbed my purse and dumped it on the table. No tickets were there, so he violently flung the purse away and scraped everything that had been in it off the table. I was sitting and holding the baby when he swung a backhand and knocked me to the floor. "What have you done with 'em?" He screamed. "Damn you, I want those tickets."

"I gave them to you, Eddie," I moaned. My lip was bleeding, and my head hurt terribly. I had held the baby safely, but he was screaming in fear. "I can't help if you can't find them. Please don't hit us anymore."

"You lyin' bitch! I know you have 'em—unless I left them at Smitty's." Eddie stormed out of the house.

When the door closed, I got off the floor and called the number that I had memorized. "Hello. I need help. My boyfriend has beaten me up again. I have to get my baby and myself away."

A very calm voice asked for my address and said that someone would be right here to pick me up and take me to a safe place.

"Instead of coming here, why don't you meet me at the store where I used to work?"

After giving her the name and address, I threw a few of the baby's and my things into a suitcase and hurried out the door. Two young women picked us up in an old station wagon and waited for us outside a law office a few blocks away.

"I remember you. You used to work in that convenience store at the corner of Twelfth Street. What can I do for you?"

"You used to come into the store when I worked there, and I knew that you were a lawyer. I need some help. My boyfriend beats me up, and I'm scared. Can you do something to keep him away from us?"

"Certainly. I can get a restraining order and have it served on him. There is a small fee for the court costs that you will have to pay."

"I don't have any money now, but if you can do something else for me, I can pay you a lot."

"What is it you want done?" He asked somewhat skeptically.

I took off my shoe and handed him a lottery ticket and a list of the winning numbers from the convenience store. He looked at them, and his eyes widened as he realized that the numbers matched. "This ticket is worth sixty-four million dollars," he said with awe.

"If my boyfriend knew that I had that much money, he would want not only a share, but all of it. Can you get me the money? I'll pay you whatever amount that you feel is fair within reason."

"You'd have to sign the ticket over to me so that I can cash it. Are you sure that you want to do that?"

"I don't seem to have all that much choice, do I? I do want you to draw up an agreement that you will turn the money over to me."

"Of course! My fee will be ten thousand dollars." He sat down at his computer, and a few minutes later, he handed me a signed document agreeing to my terms. "If you come back in a week, I will have the money."

One week later, when I returned, his office was empty. My signed document was worthless.

As I tearfully related this story later to one of the young women with whom I had made friends, an attorney volunteering at the shelter overheard the end of it and recognized the name of the lawyer who had stolen my ticket.

"I know that lawyer," he said. "Let me have your agreement that he signed." Three days later, he asked me to accompany him to the police station where I picked the culprit out of a lineup.

All good things come to those who persist.

Center of the Universe

———

We have always been told, it seems to me
The sun rises in the east and sets in the western sea.
But now we know that such cannot truly be
For the firmament does pivot round you and me.

As a stripling, on my knees, I'd peer
From father's car out the window rear
At the road sliding past; it seemed so clear
While we stood still, the spinning road did appear.

And now we probe the heavens afar
And seek answers from a distant star
Yet find that we interpret the data insofar
As reference to exactly where we are.

Milking Time

THERE USED TO BE SMALL farms in the hills, beyond the end of the power lines, where people ate dinner at midday and supper by kerosene lamp. They did their evening chores by lantern light in the winter and by evening's glow in the summer.

Chores invariably consisted of caring for livestock: milking the cows and feeding the horses, chickens, calves, and hogs. It was not an easy life, but it was not terribly stressful, and it had its pleasant moments. There was always butter to churn after the cream had been separated from the milk. The butter was stored in a little house built around the spring where it was cool in the summer. In the winter, it was kept in the "back room" where it seldom got below freezing but was never actually warm, or perhaps it was kept in the icebox, if you were fortunate enough to have one.

Vegetables were harvested in the summer and fall and either stored in a root cellar or preserved in hot-packed jars. A good summer would result in a well-stocked pantry of canned tomatoes, yellow snap beans, peas, beets, piccalilli (a tasty mixture of tomatoes, peppers, and onions preserved in spicy vinegar), and other staples. The cellar would contain a barrel of apples and a sand pile laced with turnips, carrots, and beets. There was often a barrel containing sauerkraut and perhaps a keg of hard cider.

Summer always had its moments. Sunday rides, visits from relatives, and splashing in the cool brook were memorable activities. But these were interspersed with the cutting and storing of hay, cultivating or hoeing the corn field or vegetable garden, and chasing after the cows. The hay had to be cut, in our case, with a pair of horses pulling a mowing machine with a cutter bar. Once cut, we'd pray for dry weather until the hay had cured, was raked, and loaded onto wagons. The wagons were drawn to the barn and the hay forked into the hay mow. We had not heard of baling. A warm summer day would bring out the sweat in short order, and the hay seeds would cling to bare skin whether or not we were wearing a shirt.

A fine summer would also show a barn full of hay and a silo packed with corn ensilage. It was clear that the quality of life in the winter had considerable bearing on the effort put forth in the summer.

In the fall, it was time to butcher the hogs. Usually a neighbor, or more than one, appeared, and the event took on a more gala air. First we built a fire pit and filled a large barrel with water to place over the fire. The water heated to nearly boiling while the hog was led to slaughter. After it was killed and the entrails removed, it was strung up on a block and tackle and lowered into the scalding water. Next we began the task of scraping the bristles. Once the bristles were scraped, the animal was lowered onto a table, usually consisting of several boards across sawhorses. Meanwhile, several knives had been carefully prepared and especially honed, and the hog was cut into roasts, ribs, hams, etc. I recall the process of rubbing the hams with saltpeter and hanging them in a smokehouse to cure.

Such a process would be repeated for two or three hogs, either from the same farm or from neighbors'. It was hard work but had great rewards.

Butchering a beef was much less difficult in some respects, because there was no scraping of bristles. However, skinning could become onerous. After being cut into appropriate portions, the beef was usually taken to a "freezer locker" for storing, since most small farms had neither freezer space nor electricity to operate a freezer. The beef, cut according to one's wishes, was stored in the rented locker to be retrieved as needed.

Springtime was usually the busiest time of year. Yes, fall always seemed busy with harvesting, but in the spring, there was much to be done and a short time to do it. As soon as the ground was thawed, we began plowing. There was always a need for a corn field to provide the ensilage so highly desired by the milk cows. If planning had gone well, there were calves to feed and to wean. A vegetable garden would need to be plowed and harrowed and planted. Peas, sweet corn, beans, tomatoes, squash, pepper plants, cabbage, kale, and potatoes had to be planted and cultivated. Manure had to be removed from the pit at the stable and spread around the fields and worked into the garden. The lengthening daylight was both a bane and a blessing. And oh yes, the fences required attention every spring. Not only unloved stone walls as Robert Frost said, but barbed-wire fences needed mending as trees fell on them, rust weakened them, and wildlife broke through them.

Winter provided some respite. Days were shorter and not everything could be done by lantern or lamplight. Evenings were often spent playing games or reading books by lamplight. Bed came early, not only to prepare for the next day, but to save on fuel and kerosene. Fuel often meant wood, harvested on the farm during the short winter days, to be stored up for the next winter. Usually only the kitchen and one other room were heated. The kitchen stove, with the water well on one end and ash pan on the other, kept that room warm, and often that was where we ate. The other room was heated with what we called a "Chunk Stove" because instead of the small sticks burned in the kitchen stove, this burned larger chunks of wood. If company was coming, we might open the parlor and warm it. The parlor contained a piano, and it was great fun to have Grandma play while we all stood around and sang. These were memorable occasions and were quite rare.

Of course, as the pond froze over, it was an opportunity to harvest the ice. Large cubes of ice were cut and hauled on a sled pulled by a pair of horses to the icehouse. There a layer of ice was packed, alternating with a layer of sawdust. A very cold winter provided ice to last almost all summer or into the fall. The cubes of ice not only chilled the icebox, but on warm summer Sundays, it could be chipped and used to produce rich creamy ice cream in the hand churn.

Evening milking was a time I remember well. In the fall and winter, by the light of a lantern or two, the cows were brought in from the barnyard and found the stalls into which they belonged. If one happened to step into the wrong place, its rightful owner waited patiently until we moved the errant beast to her proper spot, and then stepped in to be hitched and wait for her food. We did not have stanchions, but light chains that we wrapped around the animal's neck and slipped a pin on one end through a ring on the other.

Dad took a large bucket of grain and carefully measured out a full scoop for this animal, a half for another, and then perhaps a scoop and a half for the third. The amounts depended on the amount of milk produced, like factory workers on piecework. Grain was one of the few things that could not be produced on the farm and was costly. However, it was essential to milk production, and that determined the amount of cash income.

I recall the earthy odor of the stable mixed with frying dust motes landing on the lantern, the fragrance of the grain, and the clean smell of hay. Sometimes, when we had had a good summer and fall, we might feed ensilage, and the yeasty meal that the cows loved reminded me of the fragrance of hard cider brought up from the cellar when relatives came to visit.

Taking my three-legged stool and a milk pail that was almost too large to hold between my skinny knees, I approached my assigned cow and talked softly to her, hug close to her loins, and begin the process of extracting milk. It is a mindless activity and yet a pleasurable one. I'd lean against her side and hear the satisfying spray of milk against the pail. In the background would be the munching sounds of the cows; the shuffling of their feet; the rattling of the chains around their necks; and, occasionally, Dad's voice soothing a nervous heifer that was experiencing one of her first milking experiences. The lantern seemed to form a pattern of light and shadow, and the warmth of the animals always brought comfort and security.

I recall one of these evenings when I ventured to ask Dad about my name. It seems that we shared the first name and middle initial, but my middle name was plain old "Robert," while his was a grand "Royal." I knew that my mother would have liked to have me named as a junior, but Dad hated his middle name. "Where did your name, Theodore R. come from, Dad?" I asked.

"I was named for President Roosevelt, and so were you," he responded.

I continued squeezing the milk for a few moments, and then said, "I thought you didn't like Roosevelt."

"There were two Roosevelts," Dad responded. "We were named for the good one." So a name might affect your politics, I suppose.

During the depression of the 1930s, when money was scarce and jobs virtually nonexistent, one could not ask for a better living than a hillside farm where you grew your own food and lived in a free and open space among the wildlife and farm animals.

Passing of a Generation

Forever will the catamount hark
To the ring of the hound's glad bark;
While the hounds lead snow-shod men
Across mountain and wintry glen.

Forever will the big wily brown,
The slivery rainbow, or brookie deep down
Rise to a bright feathery hackle
And chase the flashing barbed tackle.

Forever will the band's tune ring
A caller's figures to sing,
And all the feet step in time
While the caller sounds some simple rhyme.

Forever will some farmer's ear
Ringing hammer on nail, hear;
And he'll gaze with joy at a stable
Built with pride and skill able.

And I'll lift up my eyes to the hill
And remember with sadness, yet thrill
How he taught whatever we start
To work, play, or love from the heart.

He may be gone from this mortal coil,
No longer with pain, trouble, or toil,
We've said, "Good-bye" to the body and such,
But his spirit lives in the lives he touched.

A Day of Golf

———

I LEAVE BEFORE THE SUN pushes away the night. Dressed in tan slacks and a short-sleeved shirt, I put on a light sweater. A leisurely hour's drive takes me just over fifty miles from home. My plan is that this is far enough that no one I know is likely to see me.

I am fed up with the job. I had been putting in twelve- to fourteen-hour days for several weeks, and I needed to get away. Don't get me wrong. I love my work. It's just that I am overwhelmed. I finished my report and faxed it to the main office. I know, I hadn't put in for leave, but I couldn't face going into the office today. Playing hooky is not my usual coping mechanism, but it surely feels good.

After going through my stretching exercises, I place the ball on the first tee. Looking about, I realize what a glorious day it is. I smell the morning, the newly mown grass, the sun warming the ground, the opening May blossoms. I should feel guilty, but I don't. I feel relaxed, refreshed, rejuvenated, and free. That little lie about being sick isn't going to cause me any regret. After all, I had finished the final report and dispatched it at six o'clock last night.

Two practice swings, address the ball, and let the big dog out. Nothing is as satisfying as feeling the club head's sweet spot connect with the ball. Nothing more satisfying than hearing that click that says, perfect drive. Nothing more rewarding than watching the ball soar straight as an arrow down the fairway 250 yards or more toward the green. This is going to be a great day.

My seven iron brushes the grass and strikes the ball simultaneously. Perfect! As the ball rolls past the pin, I feel a birdie coming; worst case, I have a par. The second hole, the third, the fourth—all the same. The birds are singing, and birdies are coming. I can't miss!

Even the thick, juicy Reuben and beer at the turn are spectacular. I can't stop grinning at how well my game is going. This is real medicine, rejuvenation for tomorrow's tasks. Here it is, only May, and I am playing as though I had been practicing all summer.

As I approach the tenth tee, I might as well be walking on air. I now know what people mean by "cloud nine." This is it. My arms, wrists, hips, and hands are synchronized. Every time the club hits the ball, I hear and feel the satisfying collision of the club, the ball, and the ground. Every time I swing the putter, it is such a perfect stroke that I know the ball will follow the line to the hole.

The fifteenth hole is a par three with an elevated green. It is one of the longest par threes I have ever played, 196 yards to the middle of the green. This is just over the limit of my five wood, so I consider using my three. The way I have been playing, however, the five wood might be perfect and a bit more accurate. A practice swing, a perfect address, a satisfying thwack, and the ball soars toward the hole. I can't see what happens on the green because of its elevation, but it should be near the pin.

As I approach the green, I cannot see my ball. Oh no! It must have rolled over the green. I had hit it too well. A glance to the back of the green gave no indication of the ball's location. Could it be? Could it have dropped in the hole? Could I have made a hole in one? I peek in the hole and, sure enough, a hole in one! What super luck! I feel like shouting and dancing. Never before have I made a hole in one, and this was on the toughest par three on the course. I wonder, will my name go in the course record?

But wait! No one has seen it. No one can verify it. Not only that, who can I tell about it? I'm playing hooky from work. A hole in one is for bragging, and I can't even claim bragging rights. My glorious day has turned gray. Clouds now obscure the warm sun; a chill breeze blows across my brow. The sweet taste of victory is replaced with the bitter tang of defeat.

Fifty miles west in a conference room, the entire staff is gathered around a table laden with cold cuts, fruit, and cheese as well as a rare treat, a champagne punch. A man is speaking. "Ed, as vice president, I am delighted to bring you a message of congratulations from our president. Your office has surpassed all of its goals. Your latest report, finished only yesterday by Roberts, is a crowning glory to your years' work. I had hoped to personally congratulate Roberts on his outstanding work. I hope that his illness is not serious and that he will soon be back. Please express my appreciation to him for all of his efforts. I was going to present him with a bonus check as a token of gratitude for his devoted and loyal dedication. Since I can't give it to him in person, I guess I'll just have to put it in the mail.

Life on a Silver Wing

In Memory of Colonel Dana B. Cromack

When the big guns are finally silent, and jets no
longer roar,
When big ships carry laughter, and waves gently lap
the shore,
When sentries no longer tramp parapets with arms
held at port,
And the sound of marching boots no longer echo in
the fort.

Then tyrants will no longer covet other men's
possessions,
And people will no longer fear government
oppression.
One world at peace, no fear, great dreams then men
will dare,
Of safe homes and family, of life with those they love
to share.

Not to be, say we, who served our country, ready at
the call,
Who wore the uniform of brotherhood, standing
straight and tall.
But ever men have been taxed beyond their will to
stand
Till finally they're compelled to take musket and ball
at hand.

The uniform worn has varied, to meet the nation's
call
From buckskin shirts, pantaloons, and farmer's
overall.
The doughboy in tin helmet and legs in canvas
wrapped
The flyboy's sheepskin jacket, jaunty scarf, and head
leather strapped.

And sailors in their hats so white and uniforms of the
ocean hue.
Even those in that terrible war, uniformed in gray
and blue.
The combat boots that tramped across the world's
every shore
You'll recall the images—I need not dwell on more.

Today we focus on those silver wings that few so
proudly wore
As proxies for the glistening arms held aloft by the
big jet's roar.
We think of each of those medals, pinned upon the
chest
And the terrible sacrifice they represent; awarded only
to the best.

We pause a moment on this day, and these remnants
gaze upon
And remember a brother whose breath of life too
early was gone.
But who would not change a single dream if given
another fling
For still he would seek the soaring life, life on a silver
wing.

The Marine

———

THE SILVER FRAME CAUGHT MY attention first. It was standing on a raised hearth in front of the cold fireplace. A beautiful frame, approximately two feet high and more than half that wide, it contained a picture of a marine in dress uniform. On either side of the picture was an American flag. The picture struck me as vaguely familiar, probably due to my having spent almost twenty-five years in the corps.

I had sold my small hardware store in Boulder, Colorado, last winter. Nan had nagged me to retire completely for some time, so we purchased the Titan motor home, asked our daughter to look after the house, and we hit the road.

I had asked Carl Hudson for a job in the hardware store after retiring from the marine corps when I found that I could not sit around home any longer. One thing led to another, and I finally bought Carl out and ran the store myself for nearly ten years.

I had joined the marines in 1942, immediately following high school. Following officer candidate school, I led groups of marines through more South Pacific islands than I can now recall. With a chest full of medals including the Silver Star and Purple Heart, I used the GI Bill to earn a degree in mining from the University of Colorado. When the police action in Korea broke out, I found myself back in uniform. In 1972, it became apparent that I was getting a bit too old for service in the field and did not particularly enjoy desk work, so I took my pension and settled in Boulder.

Nan and I had two children by then and were very proud of them. Our daughter became a nurse and eventually married a practicing physician. Our son was a great lineman on the high-school football team.

Now Nan and I were on our long-planned jaunt across the country. Leaving Colorado in June, we visited nearly every stateside place where I had been stationed in the marine corps and stopped at many of the tourist attractions in between. This was our sentimental journey, long-promised and long-deferred for one reason or another. At the moment, we were sitting down to breakfast in a small restaurant in the hills of New Hampshire, a long way from the rocky peaks of home.

When the waitress brought our eggs and toast, I asked about the photograph. "Oh sir, that's not a photograph. That's a painting."

"What an amazing painting," I said. "Who is the young man in the painting?"

"He's my son," she answered. "My husband and I owned this place until he passed away last year. Now my son is coming home. He has been in Iraq for more than a year."

"You must be very excited and happy to have him coming home," Nan said.

"Oh yes! I can hardly wait."

When we finished eating, we walked over to the display. Nan caught her breath, having the same reaction as I did. We looked at each other, and then back at the startling likeness in the painting. As we were paying the check, I noted that the breakfast crowd was nearly cleared out, so I presumed to ask a few more questions of the owner. "Are you from around here?"

"I have lived in this area all my life," she replied.

"And your husband, was he from here?"

"No, he immigrated from Canada. He grew up in Canada and worked for some time as a chef in Toronto, and then moved to Montreal from where he immigrated to here. Why do you ask?" she questioned.

"Oh, nothing special," I replied. "We were merely curious. Your son must have come home for his father's funeral. You said he had been gone for more than a year, and your husband passed away last year."

"Paul and his father did not see eye to eye on some things, especially the marine corps. They had not been close since Paul graduated from high school."

"When do you expect your son to arrive?" I asked.

"I'm not totally certain," she said. "He will probably be here before noon tomorrow, but it may be early afternoon. He and a friend are driving up from Boston as soon as he is cleared to leave in the morning."

Nan and I sat in the motor home and looked at each other for a long time. She finally said, "Paul! There is no way!"

"I'm sure you're right. If you don't mind though, why don't we stay over another night and drop in there tomorrow for lunch?"

World War II was the last real war where the lines were clear. There were the enemies and the allies. Ground was gained or lost, and we knew who the enemy was and, generally, where. Officially, 440,000 Americans were killed in that war, and those of us who survived returned to enjoy the largess of a grateful nation. We attended school and bought homes under the GI Bill, joined the American Legion and VFW, marched on Memorial Day and Independence Day, and made speeches at ceremonies on Veterans' Day. Our emotions were controlled, but pride beat in the breast when called to salute the flag. That was "our war." Many of us retained the sometimes blind pride of "America—right or wrong—our country."

When the Vietnam War began to heat up, the country seemed to fracture. The hippies, with their long hair, psychedelic Volkswagen vans, and loud discordant music, represented the new youth movement. It was no longer fashionable to display the flag; it was more chic to burn it. Dr. Spock's philosophy of, "Let them do as they please or you'll damage their psyche" became the banner, "Turn on, and drop out!" their battle cry.

While the generation gap has always existed, in many families, it became a chasm. Twenty-five years in the marine corps had established a rather rigid idea of discipline for me. I have finally admitted that most of the fault was mine, but when I found my son and his friends leading an antiwar rally, it was the final straw. I issued an ultimatum, "If you can't support your country, get out!"

He got out. That night, he put a few of his things in a backpack and left. A week later, his mother received a letter from Toronto, Canada. That was the last we heard from him. That was in 1974, and he was seventeen.

What does this have to do with today, 2003? That picture looked familiar because it looked like me. We couldn't believe that fate had driven us into these hills to see this picture, yet how else could one explain it? Most of our trip had been on the interstate highway system. It was only a whim that took us off the Maine Thruway and pushed us across a two-lane road in New Hampshire. We had already seen Boston and decided to avoid the major eastern seaboard cities by crossing New England into upstate New York.

We spent a restless night in our motor home in a small park near Concord. We unhooked the little Chevy, and, in the morning, we browsed in a few more antique shops and the extraordinary house of puzzles in Northwood. Finally, unable to wait any longer, we drove to the restaurant and found a table where we ordered lunch. It was not the owner who waited on us, so we dallied over a second and third cup of coffee. Still she didn't appear. Finally, I asked if the owner's son had arrived.

"He came in more than an hour ago. Ellen has been beside herself with anticipation."

Trying to hide my emotion, I said. "I'm a retired marine and would like very much to meet the young man. Do you think that could be arranged?"

A few minutes later, she returned and said, "If you'd like to walk around back, they will come down the outside stairs and see you."

Nan and I could barely contain our anxiety as we paid our bill and walked around the house to greet our grandson.

Lives We Touch

As we charge through the maze of life
Buffeted by the winds of chance,
We gain from whomever we touch
And leave with them a bit of us.

We may gain wisdom or dross
And leave behind a mere impression.
Often what we say will be lost,
But actions will last and foster.

So we watch what we do and say,
Lest unaware though we may be
As we headlong crash into a life
And impress our errors thereupon.

The Break-In

———•———

PONY STOOD BESIDE A POST in the semidarkness at the Logan Airport parking garage and watched a man park his Jaguar. The man dropped his key in his pocket and started for the terminal, and then turned and hurried back to the car. He took out his keys and popped the trunk. He looked up just as a car squealed around the corner, and he dropped his keys on the floor, thinking they went into his pocket. He removed a raincoat from the trunk, slammed the lid, and started again toward the terminal.

Pony, short for Pontonio, watched the man disappear. Pony had been filching things from cars parked in the airport by popping the locks with a long metal slat. He slinked across the aisle and looked under the Jag. Unbelievable! Here was a set of keys for the car and apparently for a house. He glanced about. Not noticing anyone around, he stepped to the driver's door and unlocked the car. He slid into the driver's seat and pawed through the glove box. The registration listed the owner and his address.

Pony sat back and grinned. What a find! He had the address of a house, and the owner had left town. If he watched for an opportunity to find the house empty, he could easily get in and become instantly rich.

"You trumped my ace! Why don't you pay attention? You do this all the time, and now we've lost our chance to set the contract." Elinor was livid, and her husband sat there with a bland look on his face. Not an unusual situation.

We have been playing bridge nearly every Thursday evening for more than two years. Elinor and Ralph always end up with her making scalding remarks. Ralph, seemingly used to it, merely said, "Sorry! Guess I wasn't paying enough attention, dear."

It was past ten, so we took our leave. The crisp October air was sweet after the stuffy house where we had been playing cards. As we wended our way across town, Alice commented on how our evenings always ended the same, yet we keep going back. Alice is my wife of twenty-five years. I'm Jim. Ralph and I were college classmates all those years ago, and we enjoy each other's company whether over the bridge table or on the golf course. I guess it's one of those fairly common situations where friendship is strong enough to survive spouses who can barely stand each other.

Saturday morning dawned crisp and sunny. I dressed in my golf slacks, my lucky shirt, and sweater; found my white country-club golf hat; and emerged in the garage, ready to take on the course. As I cruised down Country Club Parkway, it occurred to me that Ralph had not mentioned that he would see me at the course this morning.

The sun had little warmth, and a few leaves were drifting about when I parked at the country club. The scent of fall was in the air. Retrieving my putter and a few balls from my bag in the locker room, I honed my stroke where it really counted, on the green. By the time they called our foursome at 9:20 a.m., I still had not seen Ralph. Ralph seldom missed a Saturday morning golf date, but we teed off without him.

Sunday morning, Alice and I dressed for church. It seems most people seldom bother to do that anymore. Indian summer had arrived, and it was a gorgeous day, the brilliant sun replacing the murky summer haze. We cajoled our two teenagers into piling into the Lexus for the short drive to the Methodist church. Alice poked me after the first hymn to stop gaping about; there was still no evidence of Ralph and Elinor.

This is very strange, I thought. We always meet them for brunch after church, the same sort of ritual as bridge on Thursdays and golf on Saturdays. Someone must be ill. I took Alice and the kids to the Marriott for brunch but kept wondering about Ralph and Elinor.

On Monday evening I called, but there was no answer. Finally, on Wednesday, I tried Ralph at his office. He works for a consulting firm, and it's a strange place. Seldom have I talked with anyone who gave out less information. When I asked about Ralph, I was told he wasn't there. I couldn't find out whether he was out of town, expected in soon, or merely not taking calls.

Thursday was bridge day. We would definitely see them on Thursday evening, so I let it rest, though it gave me a sense of unease.

We expected them at seven. We called them at seven twenty. We called again at seven thirty. Finally realizing that they weren't coming, we discussed what we should do. It was extremely disconcerting to have no contact with a couple with whom we met two or three times a week, every week.

There had to be something wrong. I didn't quite know what to do. Their daughter lived out on the cape, and I could call her. Perhaps I should go by their house and see if there was anything there to give me a clue. Friday evening, Alice and I talked it over again and decided to call their daughter, Peggy. We left a message on her answering machine, and she called back around nine.

"I'm sorry. I haven't heard from them in a couple of weeks. I was away all last week, and, when I got back, I called and left a message at their house. They haven't called back." Peggy didn't seem at all concerned.

I still didn't know what to do. Finally, we decided to go to their house.

Their car was gone when we arrived, and there were no lights on. I rang the doorbell before noticing that the front door wasn't fully closed. "Hey, Ralph, you home?" I called. No answer. "Elinor, Ralph, anybody here?" Still no answer. I stepped into the hall and called again, louder. When no one responded, I snapped on the light switch in the hall, walked into the living room, and froze. Everything was a shambles. The TV was gone, lights were smashed on the floor, and the divan was torn apart.

I carefully made my way to the kitchen, reached that light switch, and found the kitchen was also a mess. Then I noticed something that really sent a chill up my back and caused a sudden clutch in my abdomen. In addition to several smashed dishes, there was something that looked suspiciously like blood splashed across a counter and on the floor. I turned out the lights and backed out of the room. I left the house and hurried to my car.

"You look like you've seen a ghost," Alice said. "What's wrong?" I explained what I had seen. We were both shaken. I started the car and drove for home.

"Aren't you going to do something?" Alice asked.

"I don't know," I responded. "What should we do?"

"Obviously, call the police!"

"What do I tell them? Our friends' house has been ransacked? We think they may have been harmed? How do we know? We were just nosy and walked into their house. How would that look?"

"But Jim, we can't merely ignore it. What if something is really wrong? What if they are in danger, or worse?"

"I know! Let's go home and think about this, OK?"

It was well past midnight when we finally agreed to call the police in the morning. When the dispatcher answered, I told her that it appeared there had been a break-in, and I gave her Ralph's address and my name. I didn't mention the blood. We then drove to their house and waited for the police response.

A cruiser arrived shortly, and two patrol officers approached our car. I was parked in Ralph's drive, and the cruiser parked in the street blocking me in the drive. "Did you call about a break-in?" The male member of the team took the lead.

I explained that I had stopped by to see why my friend had not appeared at golf or at church and found the door was open and the place in disarray.

"Would you show me what you found, please?" he asked politely.

After getting out of the car and starting for the door, I added, "The door was ajar, so I went in and called, but no one answer. I kept going and found everything in a mess."

As soon as the patrol officer saw the shambles in the living room, he stopped me with a hand across my chest, and we backed out the door. He then went back in and soon came out and called to his partner. They conferred for about a minute, and then she worked the radio while he came over and asked us to please wait in the car for a detective.

"What have you touched?" The detective asked us after he spent a good twenty minutes in the house.

"Only the door as I entered," I answered. "But we visit our friends here often."

"We will need to take your fingerprints to eliminate them from others found in the house. I have called in a crime-scene crew to collect evidence. I would like you to remain here for a little while longer."

Soon a van pulled up behind the other cars parked on the street. It seems that several more police had arrived and were apparently interviewing neighbors, some of whom had put on their sweaters against the October chill and were standing outside watching the activity. A person with a camera entered the house, followed by someone with a vacuum and another person with some sort of suitcase-appearing thing. The house would be getting a little crowded.

It was almost noon before the detective came back to us and asked if we would please follow him. We followed him into the hallway where the man with the suitcase was waiting to take our fingerprints. As we were milling around getting printed and cleaning the ink from our hands, the door burst open, and Ralph appeared.

"What in hell is going on?" he asked.

"Who are you?" The detective responded.

"I'm the owner of this place. Who are you?"

"I'm Detective Frank Waters. Where have you been?"

"On vacation! What's going on?"

"Is your wife with you?"

"Of course she is. Right out in the car. Jim, what is this? Why are you here? Why is everyone here?"

"We thought you were missing, Ralph," I responded. "We hadn't heard from you for a week. Your house is wrecked, there's blood in the kitchen, and…and…well, we were worried about you."

"What do you mean my house is wrecked?" Ralph exploded.

The detective then took him into the living room and on through the house. We could hear Ralph cursing and moaning.

The detective's cell phone rang as they were passing through the hallway, and he stopped to answer. "Pony! You're kidding me. OK, Thanks." He snapped his phone closed, and then reopened it and speed dialed a number. "Pick -up Pontonio Arivedo. I want him right now."

"We found the perpetrator who wrecked your house, and we'll soon have some answers when they bring that weasel in. He left his fingerprints all over the place."

Elinor burst into tears when she saw the condition of the house, and Alice tried to console her. We were about to leave when Ralph mentioned that he had lost his keys, he thought perhaps at the airport but wasn't sure.

The doorbell rang, and a patrol officer spoke with Detective Waters.

"Bring him in here!" we heard Waters say.

A cuffed and downcast Pony was brought in. Sure enough, he had a bandage on his arm where he must have cut himself while smashing the kitchen.

Dreamland

When the wild willies waken at three,
The dread dreams seem real as can be.
The heart beats in blackness of night,
Raising thoughts best kept from the light.

Like time bombs ticking away,
Not ignited in brightness of day
Yet a spark in the silence unknown
Triggers memories best left alone.

You claim you have no regrets—
Denied! Your mind never forgets.
The "couldas" and "shouldas" past
Arise from your dreams and last.

Horse Trading

My grandfather was a horse trader. There's nothing quite comparable today, though perhaps used-car salesman might be close. However, if your transportation is acting up or has traveled too many miles today, usually you take it to a dealer and make a trade. Well, that's not too much different.

Almost everyone was a horse trader to some extent, since horses were the principle mode of transportation. Grandpa was a rather sharp horse trader, but even the sharpest could get stuck now and then. Take for instance the time he traded for that pretty little roan filly. As with trading cars today, looks are important.

This filly was a beauty. Still, Gramp stood in front of her and checked out her overall shape—very symmetrical. He spoke to her, and her ears stood forward, demonstrating alertness. He ran his hands all over her legs—no protrusions, no noticeable deformities. He checked her mouth—teeth were uniformly worn off and matched the stated age. He then asked the owner to walk her around, and he watched how she moved. One more thing to do. He had to drive her to check her training and behavior under harness. Like a dream!

At last they got down to trading, and, when they shook hands, Gramp had parted with his aging bay and a small amount to boot. He hitched up the filly and drove her home, feeling very smug at the deal that he had made.

The next day, he hitched the filly to his carriage and took Grandma for a ride into the village. He even went a bit out of his way just to show off the great deal that he had made. Grandma bought a few things at the store, and they headed home. Along the way, a horsefly apparently got into the filly's ear, and she had a fit. She reared up, kicked so much that she got her hind leg over a trace, and generally thrashed around. After damaging the carriage with her kicking, she started foaming at the mouth.

Grandma was scared to death, hollering alternately at the horse and at Gramp. Gramp finally got around and held the filly's head and at last calmed her down. The harness required some repairs, and Gramp walked the horse home while a neighbor who had seen the exhibition took Grandma back in a carriage. Having seen the horsefly, Gramp couldn't really blame the horse, but he was a bit chagrined to think that he had bought such a skittish animal.

For several days, the horse seemed fine. Then one day as Gramp was bringing her out to hitch to the buggy, she seemed to have a fit again. She reared, kicked, stomped, and thrashed about until she again started foaming at the mouth. He had too much invested in this animal to just ignore these behaviors, so he called on the local veterinarian to examine her.

The vet pronounced her sound. He could find nothing wrong.

This went on for some time, alternately a gentle sweet little mare and a raging horse throwing a fit. Unfortunately, Gramp had discussed this problem rather widely among his acquaintances in town. When he decided that he had to get rid of the mare, he could think of no one who was not aware of her shortcomings. As a good horse trader, he was not above waxing eloquent about her strong points and totally ignoring any undesirable features.

He pondered this dilemma for some time before coming to the conclusion that he would have to travel quite a distance in order to make a good trade. Because he lived in western Massachusetts, it seemed quite logical that the best place to attempt a good trade would be about forty or fifty miles west in "York State."

On an early fall day, he hitched the mare to his buggy, and, crossing his fingers that she would not act up, he set out along the road west. Finding a suitable place to rest, he unhitched the mare, fed her a few oats and tethered her to graze a bit. He opened his lunch box, devoured a sandwich, and sipped some cold water from the nearby stream. After his noon rest, he again snapped on the traces and continued his journey. After crossing into the neighboring state, he sought a prosperous-looking farm and drove into the yard. Sure enough, the owner had a horse that he thought might be a good trade.

They each looked over their prospective trade: checked the teeth, ran their hands down the legs, and thoroughly examined their potential animals. The farmer then brought out a pitcher of cider, and, lighting pipes while sipping the hard cider, they began the ritual of horse trading.

It was getting dark when Gramp started for home. He was delighted that he had been able to trade that sick filly for a good sound gelding and even got a five-dollar bill to boot. He lit a side lantern and drove until it became too dark to travel. By then, he was getting rather tired so he found a small clearing and unhitched. He still had a sandwich, and a small brook provided refreshment for both him and the horse. He tied a feedbag of oats on the gelding and arranged a robe in the buggy for himself. After watering the horse again, he tethered him and, wrapped up in his robe, he went to sleep.

He awoke to birdsong at daybreak, found his way to the stream, and splashed some water on his face. His lunch box was getting like Mother Hubbard's cupboard, but he did find one more piece of johnnycake for his breakfast. The horse had another double handful of oats before being harnessed and hitched to the buggy.

By the time the sun was shining in his face, Gramp was trotting along the road in fine style and recalling how he had gotten the better of the "York State" farmer. He chuckled as he thought about what the farmer was going to say when the filly threw another fit.

Just then, his gelding began to snort, whinny, shake all over, and foam at the mouth. As Gramp jumped down to see what was the matter, the horse collapsed onto the ground, breaking one of the shafts as he did no. Before he could get to the horse's head, the horse died. Gramp was not given to cursing, but he did comment when he got home that he hoped that "York State" farmer's mother came out from under the porch and barked at him.

Music

———•———

Music is for listening;
Music is for feeling;
Music is for remembering;
Music is for enjoying;

Music may reach your ear;
Music may reach your heart;
Music may reach your feet;
Music may reach your soul.

Music makes you smile;
Music makes you sing;
Music makes you dance;
Music makes you cry.

Music may be understood;
Music may be experienced;
Music may be soothing;
Music may be stirring.

Music is for friends;
Music is for self;
Music is for now;
Music is forever.

Compatibility

"ALICE, YOU ARE COMING TO dinner tomorrow night, aren't you?" Flo, as usual, was trying to fix Alice up with a date. "Come on! We have invited this really neat guy. He's dying to meet you. What do you say?"

"Sorry, Flo, I'm not ready to get into that yet." Alice told her workmate. "You know I haven't been divorced a year yet. Let's just let it go for now."

"OK, Alice. It's your loss. This guy is just about your age, dresses nice, and has a great sense of humor. You'd really like him."

Alice felt a little guilty turning Flo down again. She had been after her to date this same guy for a month, but the divorce was too recent. They had been separated for only about a year. Forget the guilt. Back to the apartment for a "Lean Cuisine dinner," a book, and bed.

Actually, it wasn't much different than when we were married, Alice mused. *Evenings were spent waiting for my husband to come home to a cold dinner and television. Our first five years were wonderful, and then he received his promotion, and gradually the job took over his life. Well, I'm starting a new life: a new job, a new town, new friends, even took my maiden name back. Why don't I feel like celebrating?*

Alice decided it was time to catch up on a few household chores. She looked in her laundry basket and thought, *There's only a couple of loads there. Guess I'll wait until the weekend.* Her desk was a mess, but she found her unpaid bills and wrote out the necessary checks. Now that was something Randy used to do. *I hated the money part. I can't seem to even balance my checkbook,* she thought. *The heck with looks and sense of humor, I need to find someone who can add and subtract.*

Looking in the refrigerator, Alice realized that she had no fresh milk or any salad fixings. She reached into the cupboard and pulled down a jar of peanut butter, but the bread was moldy. Cutting off the moldy part of a slice of bread, she salvaged enough to stave off hunger. She spread it with peanut butter and ate it with a glass of orange juice that she had been saving for breakfast. Dropping her knife, plate, and glass in the sink to wash later, she went into the living room and turned on the television for her favorite program. She woke at eleven o'clock, stumbled to bed, and crashed.

He adjusted the knot in his tie. How could men tie a tie one time, or rather get their partner to tie it, and then merely slip it off over their heads? He would never understand their inability to tie a neat tie with the ends meeting exactly every time. This certainly was not a monumental task and was minimal in terms of appearance.

He put on his mohair jacket and glanced in the mirror. Everything was fine. Time to leave for the office. Five minutes to walk to the bus stop, two minutes until number seventeen bus, twelve minutes on the bus, and he would arrive exactly ten before nine. Even allowing for a late bus, he would always be at work before nine.

The quarterly report for his project was due tomorrow. Sally had done her job; the final draft was on his desk when he arrived. That was the only thing on his desk. His office was a model of efficiency, computer on the credenza, telephone in the top left-hand drawer. Everything else put away. He noticed that the cleaners had moved his visitor's chair again. *Why do they keep moving it up beside his desk?* He replaced it exactly three feet in front of his desk, centered so that someone seated there could look directly at him.

He placed his jacket on a hanger that he had brought from home and carefully hung it on a coatrack, also brought from home. What a mess those guys made when they hung their jackets on the backs of their chairs, say nothing about the slovenly way it looked.

He opened the bottom-left drawer of the desk and removed a plastic bag. From the bag, he removed a cloth and carefully dusted his desk, lifting up the report as he did so and placing it back exactly in the center left to right and three inches from his edge. Then he turned to the credenza next to his desk, removed the cover from his computer screen and keyboard, and dusted around it.

"Good morning, Pen!" his coworker in the next cubicle called as he passed on his way to his desk.

(*Why does he insist on shortening Penfield to Pen?* he mumbled under his breath.)

"Good morning, Franklin," he replied as he replaced the dust cloth and plastic bag in his desk and carefully folded the computer cover and also placed it in his desk drawer.

"Did you remember that you were going to join us for a little soiree tomorrow evening?" Frank said.

"Frank, I didn't agree to do that, you know. I merely said that I would think about it. I am not so sure that I'm ready to play that game again."

"Hey! Hey! I'm not pressuring you to jump into bed with anyone. I'm making it easy for you. You come to the house for dinner, and there will be an extra woman. It won't even be like a date, you know. We've got it all set up. We've tried to get you involved a half dozen times, and you always chickened out. This time you promised, well, practically promised, that you'd come along."

"Let's see how my report goes tomorrow. It's due, and I want to be sure that Alan has no problems with it. I may have to rewrite it, and that would take up much of the evening."

"Baloney! Pen, you have never had to rewrite a report. Gotta go. I'll be expecting you tomorrow evening."

He mused about the idea of seeing another woman. After all, he and Allison had been married for five years when they split up. It was a traumatic experience. He recognized that he was a slave to his work, but she knew that when they married.

Though he had been offered a better job in another consulting firm, she wouldn't even consider moving. The new job meant more money and a better chance for promotion. Of course, that all fell through when things got messy with the divorce. Still, he finally did land this job, and it was OK. The relocation also helped get through the divorce. He liked the new town and his new apartment and was getting along fine. He had developed a whole new lifestyle; used his middle name, Penfield; and things were looking up. He had his television, though he watched very little, and his books that he read a lot, so he didn't miss Allison all of the time.

Heading for home, Penfield stopped and picked up a *Times*. He was addicted to the crossword puzzle. After popping a frozen meal in the microwave and devouring it hardly without tasting it, he checked his watch, and worked through the puzzle. Fourteen minutes; not bad for a Thursday puzzle. He carefully cleaned up the kitchen, washed his utensils, and put away the clean items. He retired to his den, opened his book, and read until ten o'clock. Then he cleaned his teeth and went to bed.

"Alice, you need to get started earlier. Here it is nearly opening time, and you haven't any more than checked in! You're a good worker, but you aren't very prompt." Flo was chiding her again for not being more efficient.

Alice threw her coat at the coatrack, walked over to her messy desk, and crammed her purse into the bottom drawer. After three tries, she finally closed the drawer. *I'll have to clean out that drawer soon,* she thought. After pushing things around on her desk for a while, she said, "I have to go to the ladies' room. Will you get my phone, please, Flo?"

"Sure. I'll get it."

When Alice returned, she had straightened her hair and added a little make-up, not having had time to do that before leaving home. In fact, she hadn't slept well, thinking about whether or not to accept Flo's invitation to dinner. She didn't want to start dating. The idea seemed a little frightening, but she finally admitted that she was a little lonely.

"Why did you split up?" Flo decided to be bold as they headed into the break room for their lunch. "You never have told me, and yet you seem willing to admit that you are divorced."

"Sometimes I wonder myself why we split. Then I remember the fights about the house being a mess, dinner not on time, and his insisting on my not touching his things. I know I wasn't the greatest housekeeper in the world, but Randy was always nagging. Perhaps dinner wasn't always on time, but just as often, he wasn't there when it was ready. He was so picky!"

"Was he often late for work, or nearly late?" Flo asked.

"Heavens no! With Randolph, work came first. I came second or maybe fourth or fifth. He always got to work early and usually stayed late. A regular workaholic."

"He was working late, not seeing someone else on the side?" Flo continued.

"No. I'm almost certain there wasn't another woman. It was the job. His job was so important, he wanted to move to Tennessee when they offered him a promotion. I had friends and a life where we were living. I had a job too, maybe not as grand has his, but a job."

"Did you ever think about trying to be a little neater around the house, maybe a little more efficient?" Flo was too tactful to point out how sloppy Alice was at work.

"Sometimes I wish I had tried harder. I do miss Randy, but not his rigidity. If he had learned to be more flexible, we might have made it work, but that's water under the bridge."

"Anyhow, Alice, you are coming to dinner tonight, right?"

"I'll bet your wife just loved having you keep your house so neat, Pen!" Frank was needling Penfield as they took their coffee break.

"She kept house. I kept my den picked up and organized. We got along."

"If you got along, why did you divorce her?" Frank asked.

"Well, it's a little complicated, Frank. You see, I was doing my best to get ahead, and I was offered this great job in another city. Allison wouldn't hear of moving. Of course, there was a lot of tension at home anyhow. She was pretty much a slob about housekeeping, and she was always late."

"I can see that would be a problem. You're such a compulsive neatnik."

"Wait a minute. Just because I like to keep things neat so that I can be more efficient doesn't mean that I'm compulsive about it," Penfield replied.

"Well, Pen, old pal, you're awfully close to that." Frank changed the subject. "So, are you coming over or not? I'd better let the little lady know how many are coming to dinner."

"I'm making no commitment to date this woman you're trying to fix me up with, but I'll come to dinner. If she's a dog, I'll never forgive you."

"Great, Pen. I'll let Florence know. And don't worry, she's really very attractive."

"I'm counting on you to come to dinner, Alice. Frank just called and told me that his friend will be there, and he's dying to meet you."

"You say this guy is divorced and he works with Frank, right, Flo?"

"That's right. He's a very thoughtful and great-looking guy. He's been divorced about a year, about the same time you have. You two should get along well."

———◆———

"Honey, we're here!" Frank called as he and Penfield entered their foyer.

"I'm just pouring a glass of wine in the living room. Come on in," Flo replied.

Frank preceded Penfield into the living room and started the introductions when he noticed a startled look on Alice's face. He turned to Penfield and saw that he was staring at Alice with a shocked expression. The both gazed at each other mutely, and then suddenly both began to laugh.

"Hello, Allison," Penfield said with a grin.

"Hello, Randy," Allison responded.

Memories Packed Away

Memories packed away as in a trunk in the attic,
Taken out now and then to comfort a bad day,
Carefully unwrapped to enjoy with an old friend,
Memories hidden in the corner of the trunk.

Memories packed away, pleasant and not so,
Tucked away like a ticking time bomb,
Finding their way near the top of the pile,
Rammed back down, covered, dismissed.

Memories packed away, carefully brought out,
Ones, now and then, wished to unwrap.
Memories left buried at four a.m.,
Memories that emerge in the darkest of night.

Memories packed away until that lump,
Starting in the stomach, growing hard.
Perspiration breaking out on the body,
Regrets, overwhelming, though long past.

The Good Samaritan

He slammed the hood on his two-year-old '50 Chevy. The oil stick showed full, the radiator was up to the top, and the hydraulic brake fluid checked. "We're ready to go as soon as Pam is through work," he said to himself. Returning to the house, he again did a 'walk through' to make sure that all was neat and clean and nothing was left that belonged to them.

"The landlord should be pleased," he thought as he followed the instructions and dropped the apartment key on the table, locked the door, and drove through gathering clouds to pick up his wife from her office job.

"Christmas at home in New England!" Pam said for the sixth time, her excitement barely contained. "Did you get everything?" she asked. "How about the Christmas presents for everybody?"

"I have everything. Next stop, home in snowy New England, and then, after the New Year, Mississippi."

It was kind of the air force to permit you two whole weeks to travel from St. Louis to Biloxi."

The sarcasm was not lost on Ralph. He knew that Pam was a little homesick.

"It was nice also that you were allowed to leave at noon on your last day at work."

"You're right! I'm just happy that we're on our way."

The miles clicked by, and town after town disappeared in the rearview mirror as they wended their way along Route Forty from St. Louis across Illinois and Indiana before dark. Stormy weather was predicted, and darkness overtook them early. They were approaching Columbus when the snow began falling. Brief stops for snacks were all that slowed their progress northeastward. Plows busily tried to keep the highway open as the accumulated snow slowed them through Wheeling, West Virginia. Little traffic was evident at three in the morning. About twelve miles northeast of Wheeling, the inevitable happened. Though Ralph was a cautious driver, wind-driven snow caused a white out, and, while negotiating a curve, the right front wheel caught in the snow, and he lost control of the car. Fortunately they were traveling at a relatively slow speed; still the momentum threw the car over the edge of the road into the ditch. It lay there, tilted onto its right side.

Pam, crushed beneath her husband, had banged her head and her knee. Her husband had hit the steering wheel, knocking his breath away, and had somehow gashed his forehead. When he overcame his confusion, he found that he could get his door open and climb out on the driver's side. He helped Pam onto the road, and they stood in the snow, shivering and bewildered.

"There's a light just ahead a short way, and it seems to be a house there," Ralph said. "Can you walk that far?"

"I guess I can make it," Pam said. "My knee hurts like the devil, but it's too cold to stand around here."

As they hobbled along the deserted roadway through the falling snow, Ralph mused, "I guess we should not have sent quite as much money home to the bank. We may have trouble getting our car on the road again, unless this house is a farm and the farmer has a tractor."

"I have the forty dollars that I was just paid," Pam responded. "What do you think the tow truck will cost?"

"I don't know, but hopefully not much. I have only twenty-five dollars left for gasoline and breakfast. We probably need a doctor for your knee, and that will cost us too."

Ralph stopped pounding on the door as lights began coming on in the house. A portly man, clutching a robe around himself, opened the door. One quick glance at the bleeding head and disheveled appearance of the night visitors, and the man said, "Come in!"

"I'm Dr. Aaron. Have you been in an accident?"

Ralph said, "Yes sir. We went off the road about a half mile from here."

"Sit down; sit down," he said. "Where are you hurt?"

"I banged my head and guess I cut it on something. But my wife is having trouble with her knee. Could you look at that please?"

"Of course. Let me get my bag and put on a few clothes, if you are both OK for a minute."

He soon returned, rolled his shirt sleeves, and opened a medical bag. A woman appeared and was introduced as Mrs.

Aaron. She said, "I'll have some coffee and breakfast in a few minutes."

After checking Pam's knee, "Nothing broke merely bruised." He turned to Ralph's lacerated head. "I'll need to anesthetize that and put in a few stitches, but it appears clean and will hardly leave a scar."

"What is the condition of your car?" the doctor asked.

"It's probably OK, but it is stuck in the ditch. I'll need a tow truck."

"Would you like me to call one?" the doctor queried.

"If you would please," Ralph responded.

Francis Kazinski was born without an ounce of the milk of human kindness. He proceeded to confirm that he had not changed in his twenty-eight years. "Yer car is out front. Fender had been jammed against the tire, so I had to pull it out. It's got a rip in it. Ya owe me seventy-five dollars."

He had arrived with snow and cold at the doctor's house an hour after the call. Ralph, Pam, the doctor, and his wife had just finished a breakfast of toast, scrambled eggs, and coffee.

"I'm sorry. I only have sixty-five dollars total. Can I get your name and address, and I'll mail you the remainder as soon as I get home?" Ralph asked.

"Nope. I got the car still attached to my truck, and that's where she'll stay until I get my money."

"Just a moment," the doctor said "I'll pay your fee and settle up with the corporal."

"Don't matter none to me. I ain't in business for my health. Long as I get the money, don't care where it comes from."

The doctor paid Kazinski his money, and Ralph went out to make sure that the car was operable. It started right away and, with another little tug on the fender, could negotiate most curves.

Returning to the house, Ralph asked the doctor if he would write out his address and give him a bill for the services. The two of them could pay up to sixty-five dollars and would mail the remainder when they reached home. However, they would like to keep a little money for gasoline for the remainder of the trip.

"Don't worry," Dr. Aaron said. "There is no charge."

"But you paid the tow-truck operator seventy-five dollars. I must at least repay that much," Ralph said.

"Not to worry," responded Dr. Aaron. "He'll be needing a doctor someday, and I will get my money back."

With a grateful load off their minds, after effusive thanks, the two travelers started again eastward. Four miles along the road, they noticed the flashing lights of a police car, and, slowing, they carefully made their way around a state trooper lecturing a tow-truck driver who had apparently been speeding. They could not contain the amusement the incident produced and the irony of the situation.

"Hopefully he will be fined at least seventy-five dollars." Ralph said.

Tempted by the Trail

To Arms Academy Class of '45

By bus, they were hauled from the hills.
They came from the valleys and village.
The hallowed halls they did fill,
Anticipating kernels of knowledge.

While some were tempted by the trail,
Others were tethered to the tower.
Great dreams would falter and fail.
Great plans would perish to power.

Marriage and family a few would face,
While others dared to dream and drift.
Some ran the fame and fortune race,
While winds of war did winnow and sift.

Some would sail out on the sea,
And some would muck in the mud.
The air would attract two or three,
For the rest, the draft was the dud.

So now we yearn for yesteryear.
Rock in chosen chair, if you please,
To forget long-ago faults and fears
And rely on marbled memories.

The Golfer

———•———

HE PRESSED HIS TEE INTO the ground and steadied the ball on top. Having finished his usual stretching, bending, reaching, twisting, he swung his driver. Ever precise in all that he did, he was not satisfied with the swing. He worked his backstroke a few times until he was satisfied with it. Then he swung slowly, making sure that he fulfilled his backstroke plan and his follow-through. As a once-a-week duffer, he was meticulous in his preparation, as he was meticulous in everything.

Not pleased with his tee placement, he reached down and reset it. As he straightened up, a blond man with his bag of clubs over his shoulder approached him. It was Monday morning, and the course was almost totally vacant. The scent of newly mown grass was in the air, and a bird sang in a nearby tree. It was a great morning to be outside anywhere, and especially great to be on the golf course.

"Do you mind if I join you?" the man said.

"Not at all, but I might hold you up. I'm not a very good golfer," said the first man. Actually, people often joined him on his regular Monday golf outing. He always enjoyed company and was really not too embarrassed to play with others, since he had a fairly solid eight handicap.

"My name's Tom," the blond man said as he extended his hand.

"Call me Joe," said the first man. "Would you like to hit first?"

"No, no. Go ahead. You're already teed up, and I need to loosen up a little," Tom said as he began stretching and swinging his driver.

Joe's drive was straight down the middle about 220 yards, leaving him a 150-yard second shot for the green. Tom pulled his drive slightly and had to take his second shot out of the left rough for almost 180 yards. He left it slightly short of the green, while Joe pitched his within five feet of the pin. Joe claimed his birdie, and Tom scrambled for a par.

"You're a pretty good golfer, Joe. That second shot was fantastic, and your putt was great also," Tom commented as they approached the next tee.

"I don't remember seeing you here before, Tom," Joe said. "I play this course regularly, every Monday." Are you from around here?"

"No, I live in the next town over and just thought I'd like to try this course. I hear it is pretty challenging."

Again, Joe's drive was consistently straight and reasonably long for a once-a-week golfer. Tom hit a good drive, but missed a four-foot putt to put him one more behind Joe. And so it went for the next two holes, with Tom scrambling to keep up with Joe and only beating him on one hole.

As they approached number five, Tom suggested they make the game a bit more interesting, "Say two dollars each hole."

Joe thought a moment, and then said, "I guess I can't lose too much, I'll go along with that."

Tom still scrambled, made a long putt to halve number seven, and, by the ninth hole, Tom owed Joe six dollars.

"I've got to get some of my money back, Joe. What if we up the bet to five dollars a hole," Tom proposed.

Feeling a little more confident in his game, which seemed to be going better than usual, Joe agreed. By the twelfth hole, he now was into Tom for twenty-one dollars.

"I'm not sure what the matter with my game, is today," Tom said, as they approached the thirteenth tee, "But I think I have figured out my problem, and, to prove it, I'd like to raise the bet to ten dollars a hole."

"Wow, that's a little steep for me. I seldom even play for money," Joe said. "However, since I want to be fair to you, we can go head and increase the bet if you're certain that's what you want to do. I certainly don't want to take advantage of you."

"Very good. Then suppose we spice it up a bit more and say on top of that, we add a dollar a stroke. Will that be OK?" Tom added.

"You realize, Tom, that if we had been doing this all along, you would owe me a bundle of money. I don't want to be taking your rent money away from you."

"Oh no, Joe. I'm really feeling good about my game now, and, furthermore, I wouldn't be betting if I couldn't afford to lose."

Joe's next drive was his consistent, down-the-middle shot, even a little farther than usual, almost three hundred yards. Tom stepped up and drove his twenty yards farther than Joe's. On this par-five hole, Joe knew he couldn't reach the green in two, so he hit his consistent three wood 180 yards, leaving a twenty-yard chip and two putt. Tom followed up his lucky drive with a beautiful second shot three feet from the pin for a three-stroke eagle.

As they approached the fourteenth tee, Tom kept proclaiming that he had felt his game coming back and, in addition, seemed to have some luck also.

Fourteen, fifteen, sixteen, and seventeen left Joe down four holes and seven shots. As they teed off for the eighteenth, Joe realized how badly he had been suckered. He struggled and lost the hole by only one stroke as he looked up at Tom's big grin.

They walked off the green, and Tom suggested a cold one. Joe declined, set down his bag, and pulled out his wallet. He said, "Here's the forty-nine dollars I owe you. By the way, what do you do for a living when you're not fleecing the public?"

Tom chuckled, "I'll tell you Joe. I'm the pro at the country club in the next town over, and now and then, I like to pick up a few bucks where I can. Say, what do you do?"

Joe shook his head in disgust, "I'm a priest at St. Mary's parish, and I know better than to be betting on golf."

Tom seemed chagrined. "Oh, I'm sorry. I didn't realize that you were man of the cloth, or I wouldn't have taken advantage of you like that. Here, take your money back. I would feel really bad taking that."

"No, you won it. It will be a lesson to me."

"Well, perhaps I will come to your service one of these days," Tom said as they shook hands and started to part.

"That would be fine Tom. And why don't you bring your parents, and I'll marry them," responded Joe.

I am the Eagle

———•———

I am the eagle; I live in high country, in
rocky cathedrals that reach the sky.

—J̲OHN̲ D̲ENVER̲

I am the eagle who has achieved the great heights.
I will bear up my brothers, as God bore the Israelites
on eagle's wings out of Egypt.
I am the symbol of deeds well-done, and will forever
know that others look up to me.
In achieving this status, I acknowledge the help of
others;
My parents for their guidance, support, and love;
My scout leaders for direction, patience, and belief in
me;
My friends for their understanding and help.
I am the eagle, and I am a symbol of our heritage and
will honor God and my country.

Tonight I soar on the wings of the eagle,
Tomorrow I will strive to be the eagle!

With love to my grandson,
Eagle Scout Charles D. Cromack Jr.
Originally written for Nathan Smith's Eagle Ceremony

The Eighth Anniversary

HE TOOK EXTRA CARE IN shaving. Scraping across his chin and jawbone against the grain to be certain no shadow showed. He stepped to the closet and carefully opened a newly laundered white shirt. He fitted modest silver links into the French cuffs. His best charcoal Brooks Brothers suit, recently returned from the cleaners, was next. He turned to the tie rack and selected a deep maroon with gold flecks. A last check in the mirror assured him that he was looking his best. This was confirmed when his wife, eyes shining with pride, gave his tie a slight tweak.

With an air kiss to avoid smudging her lipstick on him, she said, "Good luck, dear, on your eighth anniversary at Franklin Associates, Mr. Associate! Are you nervous?"

"A little," he said. "I'm sure the scenario will go something like this. JJ will call me into the front office, and Ben, Alfred, and Mary Jo will be there. I'll be lectured about how we need more contracts, and that the year is not going well and other phrases intended to make me nervous. Everyone will then grin, and I'll be told that I am now a full partner in the firm, and the party will begin."

"Another possible scenario would be that JJ's secretary will call, and I will enter the front office. JJ will be the only one there. After being lectured for not producing more, developing more contacts, or whatever, I will be invited into the conference room, and the entire staff will have gathered to celebrate my eighth year and my partnership.

"Of course," he continued, "it was never a contractual clause. It was merely a promise made to recruit me away from the university. But the rumors are that a partnership is being awarded today. Who else could it be? I know JJ's girlfriend, Edna, has been given a fancy corner office, but she has only been there five years. Old Reynolds of the ragged sweaters has his eye on a partnership, but I can't believe they could promote him after all these years. Besides, it would certainly be too much of a coincidence if JJ promoted someone else on the date that my partnership was promised."

"Every indication is that my work has been outstanding. I have never had a late deliverable. So why should I feel nervous? Out of the eight years, there has never been a year when I have not obtained at least one new contract and, in many years, several. This has to be the greatest day. There can be no reason for me not to be awarded the full partnership that is called for in my employment agreement."

"I'm certain that you're right, dear. I'll make reservations for dinner, and we'll celebrate tonight."

As he drove into the city and parked his Volvo, his mind was a cauldron of expectant, exciting thoughts. Rumors had been rampant of the partnership being awarded this day.

"Morning, Frank!"

"Hi Frank, you're all dolled up today!"

"Going to a wedding Frank?"

"You're certainly looking dapper today, Frank!"

All were smiling faces as he wended his way from the receptionist to his cubicle.

"Hello, Johnson!" Donald Reynolds, dressed as a window mannequin, passed.

"Good morning." Frank froze. He had never seen Reynolds in a suit. He was a standing joke as the "scarecrow." Why would he be decked out in such unusual attire? Was that an indication of something special for him?

Pulling a folder from his work file, Frank tried to concentrate on the work. It was no use. He was too confused and nervous. When Alice brought him his coffee and the mail, she noticed his agitation. "You seem a little nervous, Frank. Do you think that your promotion is in jeopardy?"

"I've no reason to be nervous, Alice. I completed my eighth year and am entitled to the promotion to full partner. After all, that promise is what enticed me from the university. In spite of the additional money here, the university had a great many benefits: a solid retirement plan, lots of good health benefits, and the security of tenure. I remember clearly JJ saying, 'We guarantee you a full partnership in the firm, if your work is satisfactory, by the anniversary of your eighth year.' Of course my work has been 'satisfactory.' Nearly one million dollars a year in contracts, all on time and within budget."

He leaned back in his chair and smiled contentedly. Then he began to frown. "Of course there are rumors about Edna, JJ's girlfriend. She did get a vice president's office even though she has been here only five years. She may be a financial wizard, but her batting average on contracts can't compare to mine."

"JJ couldn't give her the partnership!" Alice exclaimed.

"Then there is old Reynolds. I saw him this morning, dressed as though he had just stepped out of a window display. He has been here forever but has never been outstanding."

The jingle of the telephone startled him, he waved Alice away, and, smiling, he reached for the phone. He thought, *"Show time!"*

"JJ would like to see you, Mr. Johnson."

He nervously checked his tie, buttoned his jacket, and checked the crease in his trousers, and then started down the long hallway to the front office. His somewhat eroded confidence rose as he passed each cubicle and was given a grin and a thumbs-up.

JJ, in a smart pantsuit and severe blouse, remained seated behind her desk when he entered. "Have a seat, Frank," she said, acting somewhat distracted. He grinned, albeit a little nervously, but JJ seemed not to notice and maintained her professional, businesslike demeanor.

"I want you to take over the Spruance contract, Frank. You must be about finished with the final report to the USDA," JJ continued as she fussed with some papers on her desk.

Frank's grin was still there but somewhat weakened. "That's Edna's contract, isn't it?"

"She's in over her head on that one. I know that you can handle it. I'd like you to start getting up to speed on it right away." JJ opened another folder on her desk. Frank did not know what to do. She looked up and saw that Frank was still sitting there with a much-shaken grin. "Is there something else?" she asked.

"This is the anniversary of when I joined the firm," Frank said as casually as possible.

"Congratulations, Frank! Sorry, I hadn't remembered that." Her terse response did not bode well, but he thought, *This is an act.*

"It is the eighth anniversary," Frank said beginning to lose his smile entirely.

"That's great, Frank. It seems like you have always been here. I guess we should have had a cake." JJ smiled, stood, and walked around the desk as she said this, reaching to shake Frank's hand. "We are certainly lucky to have you."

"But, I'm supposed to get a promotion, a partnership." Frank's smile was entirely gone; he was shaken.

"Oh, Frank! I guess that slipped my mind. I'll get personnel to bring me your file, and we'll go over things. Glad you have joined us, and I'm looking forward to many more productive years with you. If you would get started on the Spruance materials. We have a review of the contract very soon."

Trying to put on a casual appearance, Frank rose and left the office. His dejected demeanor, however, was apparent to everyone as he made his way back to his desk.

After perusing the contract material, he decided to ask Edna a few questions about the contract to find out what she might know about his promotion. Formulating a few questions and gathering the Spruance file, he strolled to Edna's office and knocked.

"It's open!" Edna announced.

"Would you have a minute to go over some questions about this Spruance contract?" Frank asked.

"Can we do this at the review, Frank? I'm busy right now, and the review is scheduled in the morning. It's already lunchtime, and I'll be working right through my lunch as is it."

Her imperious manner rankled, but Frank knew better than to start a spitting contest with a cat. "OK. But I assume that *you* will have the answer for JJ at the meeting." Frank gave his parting shot as he left her office.

Seething, his stomach churning, he returned to his office and tried to think of a strategy for resolving this issue. Maybe it was lunchtime, but he would prefer to find a quiet bar and drink his lunch. However, he knew it wouldn't do to get plastered before he found out what really was going on.

Try as he might, he could not come up with a strategy for resolving things. *In academe, I would have tenure and probably be full professor by now.* These were his thoughts as he reached for the telephone and called the department head at his former university. Having left a message there with the secretary, he next called a colleague in a competing firm and began the networking process.

Alice poked her head in the door. "JJ called while you were on the phone and asked for you to please join the gathering in the conference room." His heart leaped. Then he realized that this would be standard practice for awarding the promotion to anyone. He remembered Reynolds, all dolled up this morning, and Edna's brusqueness before lunch.

The hallway to the conference room was longer than it had ever been. He did not see anyone in the cubicles to give him a word of encouragement. This was the lowest of the low. How could he face his wife? Why should he continue working in this place where a contract doesn't mean a thing? Decisions were capricious, based on such irrelevant factors as friendship rather than on performance.

Finally, reaching the conference room, he paused with his hand on the handle. With extreme reluctance, he slowly opened the door.

"Come in Frank, join the party!"

He was stunned; they did remember. He was to be made a partner. They had pulled the stunt of the century, and he had fallen for it big time. Unbelievable!

"Hi Frank. Glad you decided to join us." JJ was smiling and had a glass of champagne in her hand.

"You really had me fooled, JJ." Frank responded. "This morning I was sure that you had forgotten that today was the anniversary of my joining the firm. You had me convinced that I was being passed over for partnership."

The smile faded from JJ's face. "Oh, but Frank, this isn't *your* party. Donald Reynolds has landed a plum contract with Katzenbach AG of Munich, and we are celebrating."

What a blow! He felt nauseous. He couldn't stand another roller-coaster ride like this. His eyes smarted, but he knew he couldn't show emotion here.

As he turned to slink away, JJ put her hand on his arm and whispered, "Go over and congratulate Donald, Frank. Your promotion party is following this."

If I Ever Get Old

———— ◆ ————

If I ever get old, I'll join the senior center
And reminisce about the "good ole days."
I'll play bingo on Thursdays
And have lunch there on Tuesdays.

If I ever get old, I'll speak my mind
But not complain about modern music
Nor tsk-tsk at the way youth dress
Nor regale them with tales of when I was young.

If I ever get old, I'll sit in my favorite chair
And nap now and then, and spit a lot.
I'll watch "*Wheel of Fortune*" and "*Jeopardy*"
And never complain that I can't hear.

If I ever get old, I'll take my pills and tonic
Twice each day with applesauce and prune juice.
I'll listen to the doctors and caregivers
And do whatever my significant other tells me to do.

If I ever get old, I'll relinquish my driver's license
And never tell others how to drive.
If I ever get old, I'll sit back and relax,
I'll let someone else take care of everything,
Including me.

Coming Home

————

THE RHYTHMIC CLICK-CLACK OF THE train wheels should be lulling me to a restful place; however, my mind is much too restless. I smell the mixture of diesel fumes and cleaning chemicals and am reminded of earlier train rides. Why am I taking this trip? I know that I sent in my name as a race participant, but I now believe that it was a stupid thing to do. Yes, I admit some yearning for visiting the place where I grew up, but also reluctance to return, to see the people, the dread of how they will look at me. Perhaps this fear is groundless; they may not even remember me. After all, it has been nearly twenty years.

Twenty years ago. Who could forget? I could throw a baseball. Our high-school team was tied for the state championship. The whole town was excited. I had that letter from Pawtucket. As soon as graduation was over, I was off to camp for Triple-A ball. As a star baseball player headed for the big leagues, people I didn't even know would smile and say, "Hello, Carl." Intoxicating for a seventeen-year-old youth. The accident had nothing to do with them; it had no effect on them, but they resented me for it. Oh yes! I resented it myself.

Nan and I were queen and king of the prom. Life was about as good as it could get. Then the accident. That was a dream career down the toilet. I didn't believe it at first, but after my arm healed, I realized that I would never be able to throw a baseball ninety miles an hour again.

The sensations of the railroad reminded me clearly of that July trip following high-school graduation.

Boarding the train at six in the morning, not mentioning my plan to anyone but my parents, I headed west. My arm had healed, but my mind dwelled on that tragic night. Fortunately, I had dropped Nan off at home and only had six miles to go to my house. The sun was soon to be pushing over the hills, and I was exhausted. I just didn't know it. My eyes couldn't have been closed more than seconds, but that's all it took. The right front wheel caught in the soft shoulder, and the car flipped over. Somehow I received only a bump on my head and a shattered arm. Fortunately, I wasn't speeding. The broken arm was the disaster. My pitching arm. When the arm healed, it was obvious that I would never pitch baseball again. Like a puppy with its tail between his legs, I fled my home town and enlisted in the army.

Why am I coming back now? It doesn't make sense. No sensible person would return. My ego seems to be in the way. Since the army released me, my life has revolved around racing, and this place has one of the premier races in this part of the country. Of course, I have to admit there is some hometown attraction drawing me, but it is more like what the psychologists call "approach avoidance"—I'd like to return and show people I'm not worthless, but what if they ridicule me or perhaps just ignore me? Not sure I can stand either.

The army didn't mind the weakened arm. I could still tote a rifle, so off I went. Then it was typical army: periods of training interspersed with periods of boredom. To overcome the boredom, I kept up a rigid physical regimen. When the opportunity arose, I volunteered for Special Forces. More training, more rigorous, and shorter periods of boredom. As a staff sergeant I led a raid during Gulf I. As a result, after returning stateside, I was promoted to technical sergeant and led men, but mostly in training.

Meg was a nurse, first lieutenant, stationed at Fort Bragg where I was training. I didn't find out that she was an officer until two or three weeks after we met. We met in town and seemed to hit it off at once. We were married six months later. This was the first time I had found happiness since high school.

Then came the second invasion of Iraq. We learned such terms as IED (improvised explosive device), and we watched our comrades get blown up. The first tour was hell, though hell might have been cooler and less hectic. As Special Forces, we were in the heaviest fighting most of the time. When I returned stateside from that tour, I learned what PTSD (post-traumatic stress disorder) stood for. Our son was one year old, and we were soon to have a second child. I had every reason but one to remain stateside—my buddies were dying in Iraq. After some fairly intensive therapy, I felt that I had my head on straight again and volunteered for a second tour.

My duty assignment this time was primarily administrative. The Green Zone was well protected and Meg was pleased that I would be safely situated in Baghdad. Ha! On my way as a courier with highly classified documents to be delivered to a unit in the field, I came upon a crowd gathered in the street and, after stopping, realized that a group of soldiers was being harassed by a number of unarmed civilians. The men had orders not to fire on unarmed civilians unless confirmed that they were suicide bombers. As I attempted to intervene and move the soldiers away from the Iraqis, I chanced upon an IED. My life changed again.

Walter Reed Hospital was destined to put me back together, at least as much as possible. Hours of surgery, hours of rehab, hours of counseling; depression is most difficult to overcome. I had always had physical strength and boundless energy. Somehow I overcame the dreadful pain to both body and mind. I was soon spending every spare minute in the gym. I was bound to regain my strength. Before being discharged from the hospital and the army, I began channeling my energy into racing. With the support of Meg and my children, I set out to race in every venue offered. It was this obsession that was pushing me back to my hometown.

I knew that my plight had resulted in some publicity, but felt sure that it was localized. Whoever reads about awards of medals or results of combat casualties unless directly, personally affected? So I felt confident that at least that would not be part of my welcome, if it would be a welcome, when the train stopped. For sure there would be people at the station, for the race was a sufficiently big deal that the train was making a special stop. In fact, it was a special "race train" to bring people to this particular place for this particular race.

The rhythm changed. We were slowing for the station. My stomach tightened, and my pulse increased. "*Stop it!*" I thought. Why should I have such a reaction? I came to this event of my own free will, and therefore whatever happened, happened.

As the train slowly rolled to a stop, I looked out the window and saw a sea of faces. Either the town had grown, or a lot of visitors gathered to greet the train. Some were holding signs, but I couldn't see what these placards said.

As *I descended from the train, a roar arose from the crowd. Then I saw the large banner, "Welcome home, Carl! Our home town hero!"* I couldn't believe my eyes and ears.

A band struck up a march, and a man approached me. "Remember me, Carl? I'm Joey, your best friend from high school. I'm the mayor now, and I want to welcome you to our town and present you with a key to the town." Tears filled my eyes.

"Why are you doing this? What's going on?" I stammered.

"Carl! You're a hero. Don't you know that? You've put our town on the map. Not only are you a hero from your service in Iraq where you lost your legs, but a racing figure of national prominence. We are all so delighted that you have chosen to come here, not only to race, but to visit us and to honor us with your presence."

I could hardly believe that this wasn't a dream. Meg, my son and my daughter stepped up and touched my shoulder and began pushing my wheelchair through the crowd as people reached out to shake my hand.

All Living Things Are Born to Die

From somewhere deep in our hearts,
We know, all living things are born to die,
Yet when it's time for us to part
We do so with longing soul, and sigh.

We cling to life with tenacious grasp,
Loath to leave this mortal coil.
Though wracked with all from life's long past,
We must be finished with this earthly toil.

Now with renewed life we start
To mend our sorrow and say good-bye,
And echoes again within our heart
All living things are born to die.

A Brief History of the Shelburne Church

"HERE IS THE CHURCH. HERE is the steeple. Open it up, and see all the people."

This children's ditty went through my mind when we returned to the First Congregational Church of Shelburne in 1993. Having left a suburb of Washington, DC, and a church of nearly all retired people, we were amazed at the large number of young families.

Yet the Shelburne Center Church is much more than these young people. It represents an historic landmark for the town, a beacon for travelers along the Mohawk Trail, and a truly centering influence in the community.

Celebrating its 225th year in 1995, this church has survived difficult times and brought happiness to many people. Its first pastor agonized for more than a year on whether or not God really called him to minister in the "backwoods of Shelburne." Reverend Robert Hubbard, the first settled pastor, finally accepted the position in 1773. He preached in the Daniel Nims home before the frame church was built on Old

Hill in 1773 to replace the log meeting house that had been built in 1769. Today several newer homes are situated on Old Hill, along with the church's original graveyard.

A church was a significant element in colonial times because a town could not be incorporated until a church was formed with a settled pastor. In many ways, it served as the court, with the pastor as judge and the members as jury. The story of a church member who was accused of stealing corn can be found in the church archives. Though the church found him not guilty, when the pastor announced the verdict he added, "Brother Freeman, the church has cleared you, but, for my part, I believe you stole that com." Shortly after the trial, Mr. Freeman brought his child to be baptized. During the ceremony, the minister was heard to pray, "that the child might never put his hand to his neighbor' goods."

The frame church on Old Hill was demolished in 1832, when it became too small and unsuitable to the congregation's needs. There was considerable disagreement on where to build the new one. Those who wanted it rebuilt on Old Hill arranged to have the lumber delivered to that site. One night before the building commenced, the lumber mysteriously moved from there to where the church presently sits, next to the Mohawk Trail in the midst of Shelburne Village. There it was dedicated in 1833. Controversy continued. Some insisted there be no steeple on the new building, while others felt strongly that a steeple was needed. One member was reported to announce, "If there is a steeple it should look to heaven. If not, it will look like hell."

That structure stood for only twelve years, however, as it burned during Sunday services on March 9, 1845. History has it that on the Sunday morning when the church burned, a Baptist preacher was to deliver the sermon. Before he delivered the morning message, some pipes overheated and caused a fire. The congregation fled, but not until they finished the hymn. Some members voiced the opinion that the conflagration was an act of God in retribution for allowing a Baptist preacher in the pulpit.

The existing structure was dedicated in December, 1845, and has been pointing its spire toward heaven for more than 150 years.

Reverend Hubbard served the church until his death in 1788. Following several temporary pastors, a minister by the name of Jesse Townsend was called and served for the five-year period from 1792 to 1797. One of the most beloved pastors of the church was Reverend Theophilus Packard, holder of a doctor of divinity degree, who served the church from 1799 until his death in 1855. His son, Reverend Theophilus Packard Jr. served from 1823 to 1853 as copastor with his father. Theophilus Jr. was not the only minister trained by his father. Reverend Packard Sr. was credited with preparing thirty-one students for the ministry. It is almost unheard of today to find a minister serving a church for fifty years.

Even Reverend Packard had his foibles, however. It is told that it was his habit to leave a harness on his horse night and day. Some of the younger townsmen were quite upset over this practice. Because Dr. Packard continued to "mistreat" his horse in such a fashion, the young men of the church decided to teach him a lesson. When the good reverend prepared to leave for church one Sunday morning, he discovered his horse unharnessed. In fact, the harness was missing. Upon arriving at church that morning, he discovered the harness draped across the pulpit.

A church vestry was built near the church in 1847. It served for many public functions—including town meetings—and contributed greatly to centering the community on the church. Its availability for a multitude of activities drew the people of the community like a magnet. During my youth, I remember the weekly dances, minstrel shows, plays, and concerts. It was also the grange hall and hosted a variety of meetings.

When the vestry was declared unsafe for public gatherings in 1959, it was voted to lease the unused center schoolhouse for vestry purposes. Formerly known as the Consolidated School, the building ceased to be used when a Union School District was formed, and children were bused to Shelburne Falls. Soon after leasing the building, the church voted to purchase it and, in 1962, remodeled and renamed it the First Congregational Fellowship Hall. Today it serves the same purpose as the former church vestry had: a meeting place for a multitude of activities, a church school for the youth, and grange hall. It remains the center of the community.

As recently as the 1960s, there was a distinction made between "members of the church" and "members of the parish," no matter their religious affiliation (or lack thereof). This distinction may have created some occasional dissension, but it also contributed to drawing the entire community to the church. An ongoing example of the overlap between the church and the parish is the annual Christmas pageant, a tradition now for almost sixty years. It is held in the church, yet participants include children of all members of the community, whether Roman Catholic, Protestant, or unchurched. Vacation Bible school is provided each summer and is eagerly attended by younger community members who may never be seen in church the rest of the year.

In the early days, it was customary to "line" or "deacon" a hymn as it was sung. There were strong feelings aroused over the introduction of musical instruments in the church, even the conservative bass viol, violin, melodeon, and organ. There was such contention over the music in the church that one minister was said to regret that he ever came to town.

In 1915, George E. Taylor donated the beautiful pipe organ installed at the front of the church. The pulpit was moved forward to allow the choir to sit behind the preacher. A shed added to the back of the church provided room to install the pipes for the organ. This room may be entered through a door from the outside or from a very small opening in the choir loft. In the 1940s, two young boys, one reportedly the minister's son, crept in back of the organ and moved the pipes about. On Sunday morning the organist discovered the results of this mischief. A choir member crawled through the small opening of the choir loft and rearranged the pipes in their correct order.

A community church will always have disagreements. In recent history there is the story of the fir tree in front of the church. A very attractive addition when it was small, the tree had grown to where many felt it should be removed. Some, however, resist change of any kind. After weeks of sometimes strongly stated opinions, two of the church members decided to take matters in hand and removed the offending tree one night. The next Sunday, they awaited the outburst, but no one seemed to notice that the tree was missing.

In any organization there are "doers" and "complainers," and sometimes they switch roles. Yet differences notwithstanding, everyone comes together to respond to a need. A member of the church annually made and sold apple pies over Columbus Day weekend. This was her source of income for paying the property tax on her small gift and antique shop. When her husband was suddenly struck with a terminal illness in September, she had to give up her "pie season." The church and community baked and sold nearly four hundred pies in two days and donated the money to the family. It seemed that everyone helped by donating and peeling the apples, baking and selling pies, and even delivering them when requested.

Perhaps the most lasting impression and, in some cases, the only impression of the church, is the magnificent church spire. Blown off in 1916 by a high wind, it was soon replaced. Lighted since the early 1950s, day or night, this tower provides inspiration to those motoring along the Mohawk Trail eastward or westward.

The picture-perfect location and clean lines of the rather austere building have caught the eye of thousands of tourists. It is an often photographed scene and has been captured on canvas in oils, acrylics, and water colors to say nothing of several variations of notepaper containing line drawings of this structure. No matter whether it is framed in pale greens of spring foliage, by the azure summer sky, in pastel reds and oranges, or with diamond-like ice crystals, the church, photographed or painted, reminds people from Europe to the Orient of a New England village.

The history of the First Congregational Church of Shelburne does not stop somewhere in the past. It is a living force in the life of our community and the world today.

As in the past, the church today faces problems. The buildings—parsonage, sanctuary, and fellowship hall—are all showing their age. The church spire recently lost the siding from one side due to wind, and desperately needed painting. The congregation of young families, often struggling to make ends meet, can generally pledge barely enough to cover ongoing expenses. A capital campaign was undertaken to refurbish the church building and, most specifically, the magnificent steeple. A church that struggles to meet a very modest operating budget pledged nearly double that amount to renovate the church. These same people recently called a new pastor and, prior to his arrival, refurbished the parsonage, not a small factor to weigh in favor of a pastor thinking of serving this church. Much of that financial burden was the direct result of the very generous contribution of a large portion of the interim minister's salary.

With a new pastor igniting the imagination of the congregation, the members continue to reach out to the community and to finds ways to serve and to grow. The growth is not only in members, but in commitment and stewardship. As a renovation project is transforming the sanctuary, people are talking of the need to refurbish fellowship hall and to serve larger needs such as Church World Service and support of world missions. Yet all is not roses. No progress is without a struggle. There are those who feel that our first responsibility is to the local church, while others see world service as essential to their faith. Any change that is proposed in the local church finds its detractors as well as supporters. As long as there is honest differences and communication, dialog is good.

The rhythms of life are different today. Whereas earlier livelihood came from the land, now many work in the city. Tensions exist in how quickly things are done, whether making do is good enough, or whether it should be done to some different standard. In the future, rural Shelburne will become more of a bedroom community. New houses are going up for people who will be holding jobs in town. Within this church, there is a greater diversity of beliefs than most. Despite differences, despite struggles to make ends meet, this small rural church continues to be a vital, vibrant, and essential center of this community.

(This paper, written in the mid-1990s, continues to speak today, as we again undertake a capital campaign with the aim of insulating our buildings, reducing our use of oil and electricity, and remodeling our kitchen.)

BIBLIOGRAPHY

History and Tradition of Shelburne, Massachusetts (1958).

Reverence Theophilus Packard Jr., *A History of the Churches and Ministers and of the Franklin Association* (Boston: 1854)

interviews with church members

A Father's Thoughts

What do you say in a word or phrase
When chattering or yakking in a meaningless way?
Words come easy when we've little to say.
"Got to go now! Have a nice day."

But sometimes they gather in the back of your throat.
There's something in your mind that seems to float.
It wants to come out, but the thought's so large
It catches and gets hung, like a beached barge.

These unsaid thoughts with feelings so strong
Can get bottled up and held too long.
Perhaps it's emotion that blocks the mind,
Or maybe it's mere words we can't find.

Take a man whose children are now all grown.
He didn't take time for them to be known.
Now to them he would say, right out loud,
He loves them all; they've made him proud.

But he can't say the words; they sound so odd.
Composed in his mind, he stands like a clod.
"Hope everything's fine; are you feeling well?"
Instead of saying what he really should tell.

Homeless

———————

HE RELUCTANTLY LEAVES HIS NEST and ventures into the cold, snowing evening. Pushing his cart, he moves up the grade from the railroad tracks and begins his daily trek along the street. "Nobody better take my home," he mumbles half aloud.

He pauses at each trash barrel along the street and paws through it, searching for anything that might have some value, at least in his mind. A scrap of material, a half-eaten sandwich. He moves on.

A matronly lady, wrapped in muffler and fur coat, approaches, and he continues along his way. His mumbling disturbs the lady, and she veers off to avoid nearing him. Two teens are enjoying the snowy evening with their fancy ski outfits and tasseled toques. He aims his cart at them and mumbles louder, something that sounds vaguely like a feral animal. The teens shout, almost in unison, "Watch it, you stupid bum!"

He is now shivering from the cold, so he decides to step into the pizza parlor. It is a place where he can watch his cart to make sure nothing is stolen from it. Stepping inside, he attempts to brush some of the snow from his ragged coat. The manager, recognizing him from previous encounters and wishing to assure his customers' comfort, tells him to move along. He mumbles incoherently but edges toward the door.

A mother and daughter, enjoying a pizza and beverage, ask him if he would like a piece of pizza. He reaches out a grubby hand and takes the proffered morsel, but the manager is still urging him toward the door.

He steps out, allowing a gust of snow to slip in through the door. The frigid weather hits him in the face, and he moves toward his "home." Back down the slope, he nears the railroad tracks, and, with a cautious eye out for authorities, he scampers into the tunnel and finds his nest. He is still cold but at least out of the snow and wind.

Soon he is joined by two others who wish to share some of his space. At this point, he is so cold and numb, he doesn't object. Soon the cold and snow are no longer of concern, and he is left to be found by a railroad track worker in the morning.

"Got a job for you," grizzled senior detective Sean Murphy said when Mona stood shaking the snow from her hat after returning from peacefully settling a domestic disturbance.

"OK, Sarge, but I hope I have a chance to warm up a little first," she said.

"Oh yeah. You can do this right in the office," he said with an evil grin.

"Uh oh! What evil task have you dreamed up for me now?" Mona Evans was a newly minted detective. She had spent four years as a patrol officer and had shown herself to be able to lead as well as take orders. There had been some resentment by the older officers when she was made detective so soon, but she proved herself more than capable. Still, they often found the least desirable jobs for her.

"There's some trash bags by your desk. Figure out who the contents belonged to and how to reach the next of kin. He was another bum frozen to death last night. Should be a piece of cake, pun intended," Murphy said.

Mona walked over to her desk and opened a bag. An unpleasant odor assailed her nostrils, but she made a face at Murphy's back, and pulled on a pair of latex gloves from her desk. The first thing she looked for was a wallet of some sort, which meant overcoming the stench of urine and searching through the trousers. Among a pile of worthless scraps of paper, she found a smeared and barely legible driver's license that had expired two years before. She made out the name Arnold Oxman. Realizing that this could be another worthless scrap that had been discarded by someone else, she didn't immediately assume that the victim was Arnold Oxman.

Painstakingly examining everything in the first bag, she made a list of every item that was not obviously worthless junk, which was a very short list. She then tackled the next bag and proceeded in the same fashion. She lifted out some sort of box wrapped in a rag. She unwrapped it and found a carefully preserved box containing a Purple Heart and a Silver Star medal. These are not things that people throw away. Where had this person gotten them?

Removing her gloves, she walked over to the coffee pot and poured a cup of the vile liquid. Her mind was not on the coffee but on this unknown John Doe. "Hey Sarge," she said as she walked by his desk. "Has the M. E. printed this guy?"

"Don't know. Call him up and ask him. Why, have you found out who he is?"

"I have a possible, but I think he was a vet, so the prints should give us an ID," Mona said as she wandered back to her workplace and sipped her coffee.

She picked up the phone and punched in the number for the medical examiner. Betty answered the telephone and, in response to Mona's question, said, "Sure, we have his prints. You want to come get them?"

Mona pulled her coat on and signed out for the morgue. This was becoming a more interesting case than she originally thought. Sure lots of vets turn up to be homeless, but this guy was some sort of hero, if those were his medals. It was highly unlikely that they were trash that he had picked up.

"Your prints came back. The guy's name was Arnold Oxman," Murphy greeted Mona when she arrived for work the next day.

"Thanks, Sarge!" Mona replied. Google seemed like the fastest way to identify this guy by more than a name. An immediate hit reported that an Arnold Oxman had been a major in the army during the Gulf War. He had been highly decorated, including the Silver Star and Purple Heart that Mona had found. "Damn shame he ended up homeless," Mona mumbled to herself.

Also listed under Oxman was a Julia Oxman, who had written a number of articles in scientific journals as a professor of science at Ohio State University. *Oxman is a rare name. Could this be a relative?* mused Mona. Further research showed that Arnold had been employed by an aerospace firm in Georgia, where he had also written professional articles in a number of journals. Too much of a coincidence, thought Mona.

Old fashioned detective work led her to the telephone directory, albeit an online version, and the telephone number for Ohio State University. The automated directory suggested she try listings for "O," and, sure enough, there was Julia Oxman, or at least her voice mail. Mona left a brief message and asked Ms. Oxman to call her.

Mona's report on the deceased was slightly longer than many, because she felt compelled to include pertinent military history. When the telephone rang just before lunch, Mona was pleased to hear Julia Oxman's voice.

"Who are you?" asked Julia.

"I am Detective Mona Evans of the Watkins, Massachusetts, police department. I wonder if you are you related to an Arnold Oxman?"

"Yes. What has my father done now?" Julia responded in a somewhat disgusted tone.

"Ms. Oxman, I'm sorry to have to inform you that he has died," Mona said.

"Are you certain that this is my father we are talking about?"

"Is your father Arnold Oxman?"

"Yes! But why is he in Massachusetts? He lives in Georgia. There must be some mistake."

"Would it be possible for you to come here to identify him?"

"How did he die?" Julia finally asked.

"He died from exposure. The temperature here has been in the single digits or even below zero," Mona explained.

"I can't believe that it's my father. I'll get a flight out right away. There is no way that it could be my father, but I'll look at him."

When Mona hung up the telephone, she was puzzled at the strange conversation she had just had with Julia Oxman. They must have been estranged for Julia not to have known that her father was homeless. Further, she seemed to find it impossible to believe that he was dead. *I can't wait to meet this woman and learn the story behind Arnold Oxman, military hero, father of a professor, and homeless bum.*

"I'm looking for Detective Evans." Mona heard the brusque voice spoken to Sergeant Williams at the front desk and rose to go out and greet Julia Oxman.

"You said something about exposure. Are you saying that this person froze to death?" Julia asked as she and Mona were on their way to the morgue.

"Yes. That is the recorded cause of death," Mona said.

"How the hell could someone freeze to death, in spite of the cold weather? here are heated vehicles, motels, and offices. Since you're involved, I assume that he had been mugged and left to die somewhere. Or was he drunk and fell down, or what?"

"Let's confirm that it is your father, and then we'll go into more details."

As the medical examiner prepared the body for viewing, Mona and Julia waited quietly in his office. When he was ready, he invited them into the cold morgue and carefully uncovered the victim's head. Julie, gave a gasp and shiver, and then turned away and walked back to the office. Mona followed, nodding to the M. E. in response to his questioning glance, indicating that there was no doubt that the body was the woman's father.

"Tell me more about how he died," demanded Julia.

"I'll tell you, but first let's go somewhere and get a cup of coffee or tea or whatever you wish, but let's get out of this place," Mona said.

Sitting in a booth at Denny's with a cup of coffee and donut, Mona began explaining what she knew. "Your father was homeless and—"

"Homeless!" exclaimed Julia, "He had a beautiful ante-bellum home near Atlanta and a solid job with a good salary. He and my mother had paid for my education and had never wanted for anything. What do you mean, homeless?"

"I don't really know why, but he was living near the rail-road tracks, under the street. He had obviously been on the street for some time. Can you tell me when you last saw him?"

Julia was silent for some time, and Mona waited her out. Finally, she took a deep breath, sighed audibly, and began to talk. Her eyes filled with tears, but she made no attempt to wipe them. "My mother died four years ago. My father and I never got along. I hated the military and expressed that in every way I could. He wouldn't argue with me about it, but he shut me out of his life. Once Mother had died, I never saw my father again. I didn't realize that he wasn't still working and living in Georgia."

"Do you have any idea what caused him to go onto the street?" Mona asked.

"No, other than Mother's death hit him very hard. At her funeral, he was nearly catatonic. Someone had to lead him around, as he seemed unable to think what to do. I know that he loved my mother very much and that she, to a large extent, managed his life. With her not there, he must have decided to give up everything. I assumed that he would pull himself together and that he would still be working on war machines in Georgia."

"Is that why you didn't see him again, his 'war machines'?" asked Mona.

"I guess. I didn't visit him because we were strangers, and he had written me off. I don't know why I didn't try to overcome our estrangement, but he didn't either. It's terrible that he ended up a destitute and homeless man."

"I guess that my involvement in this affair is finished; however, I'd like to learn more about his life, because it seems so strange. Would you be able to tell me what you know, or is it too painful?"

"Is there a good, reasonably priced motel near here where I could stay tonight? I'd probably feel better telling about his life and maybe find some way to live with my guilt over ignoring him."

Mona agreed to meet Julia for dinner at six thirty, and they parted with a little better understanding than when they had met.

After enjoying a glass of wine and ordering their dinner, Julia began to relate what she knew of the history of Arnold Oxman.

Raised in a small suburban town near Atlanta, Arnie was an *A* student. He applied himself not only to his studies but also to sports. As a first-team quarterback, he had no difficulty being accepted to West Point. Cadet Oxman, while top in his high-school class and *A*-team high-school quarterback, found competition in the corps was far more challenging. He struggled at times but graduated in the top 20 percent of his class.

Following graduation, Oxman married his high-school sweetheart, Lydia Wellman. She was the daughter of the president of a large manufacturing plant in Georgia. Like the other army wives, Lydia followed Arnold around in his assignments, even though she often saw him only briefly while he was participating in training, and then less often when he went into combat. When Julia was born, Arnold was in airborne training and was confined to the post, unable to see his wife and daughter for several days.

Second Lieutenant Oxman finished airborne training and then rangers. He was highly competitive and was often in the middle of action in the near East. His promotions came rapidly, and his chest filled with medals. When Julia entered college, Oxman was a major and assigned to the Pentagon. He was in Iraq when she graduated with her bachelor's degree, and in Afghanistan when she was awarded her doctorate.

"I can't tell you much more," Julia said. "We rarely saw each other or spoke after he returned. I do know that he had been wounded and was invalided out. He was avidly sought after by government contractors for his knowledge of combat and combat equipment. He took the job in Atlanta, and I moved on in my career."

"Would you know any of his contacts in Atlanta?" Mona asked. "While I have no official need to know, I would like to know how he ended up on the street, especially after your explanation of his financial situation."

"I don't know anyone, but I could call his company and maybe one of his neighbors. My mom was quite close to an Alice Waters, next door. If she's still around, she might know something about his situation."

"Would you mind if I listen in when you call?" Mona asked.

"It's too late to call the company, but it might be a good time to reach Alice. Shall we go to your office, or would you like to come to my room?"

"Why don't we go to your room and place the call from there. If there's no answer, you can then leave a call back," Mona suggested.

"This is Alice."

"Mrs. Waters, this is Julia Oxman. Do you remember me?"

"Of course, Julia. How nice to hear from you. Are you in town?

"No, I'm not. I hate to bother you, but do you know what happened to my dad?"

"Oh Julia, I don't, and I have been so worried. His house is now being auctioned off for taxes. No one has seen your dad for a long time."

"Do you know how long?"

"Oh, I think it was very shortly after your mother passed away. He just disappeared. For a while, I used to try to keep his place neat, and I picked up the newspapers and mail. Then finally it all stopped coming, and I'm sorry to say that I haven't kept the place as neat as I should."

"It wasn't your responsibility, Mrs. Waters. It appears that my dad just left everything and went to live on the street. I can tell you that he has now passed away up in Massachusetts. He had that beautiful home in Atlanta but preferred to be homeless. I don't understand." Julia was in tears.

"I'm so sorry to hear that he has passed away. Is there anything that I can do?"

"No, Mrs. Waters. Thank you for your help. I'll be back in touch with you." Julia hung up the telephone.

"Did you get all of that?" Julia asked Mona.

"Yes. It seems so strange. Will you try to reach some of his coworkers tomorrow?"

Mona was clearing up paperwork in the office when she heard Julia come in the next morning near noon. After inquiring about her evening, Mona asked if Julia would like to go to lunch.

They each ordered soup and a salad, and then Julia began to explain what she had learned from the company where her father had worked in Atlanta. She had reached his office mate Brady, as well as his supervisor. The supervisor had merely said that her father had failed to show up for work, and, after no communication with him though many attempts had been made, he was terminated.

The office mate was far more sympathetic. He had gone by, following her mother's funeral, and spent some time with her dad. Her dad had told Brady that he couldn't understand what was happening. In fact, he had seemed very confused. He told Brady that he needed some time to absorb all that had happened and that he was going to have to get away for a while. Brady went back the next day, and her dad was gone. They never heard from him again. The only clue Brady could offer was that he had said that Lydia was his whole world, and he had no idea how he would live without her.

Mona absorbed this information and finally offered, "Your dad was a military hero who could face enemy fire repeatedly but could find no way to face the loss of his wife."

"I know," Julia replied. "And I should have been there to help him through that crisis."

Birthdays

Kodachrome of October
Becomes white and black of December.

And November's stuffing
Becomes January's Lean Cuisine.

While hearts of February
Become April's fool.

Flowery May baskets
Turn into June's I dos.

And July, red, white, and blue
Fade in dog days of August.

While September's cool breezes
Turn the calendar once more.

And a candle wish
Adds one more year.

Valentine's Day

I SIT ALONE, TIRED OF the television shows, tired of the DVD happy endings or the make-believe crime, tired of life. I realize that I am wallowing in self-pity, but depression can't be sloughed off that easily.

What could I have done differently? How could I have been so blind? Some wit once said that if life hands you lemons, make lemonade. I can only think of that tune about how pretty the lemon tree may be, but the lemon fruit is impossible to eat.

There must have been a clue that this would never last. There must have been something that I missed in our relationship. Yet, we were so happy. She laughed at my corny jokes. We were lost without each other. We both loved the same music, the same movies, and the same food. I can't recall a time or an incident that would have provoked her leaving.

The desolation is unbearable. I think I shall do something drastic. I can't bear this any longer. I feel like that situation I heard of where a man walked out into the ocean and kept walking or swimming until he could no longer return to the shore.

Well, here I am on the beach. There is the ocean, and it is calling to me. I only have to start walking. One step at a time until I no longer feel the pain in my heart. The water is warm this evening, and I can begin to feel the comfort of the ocean, caressing me and welcoming me.

"Help!"

Where is that call coming from? It sounds like someone in trouble.

"Help!"

There it is again. Someone is desperate. There she is. A woman is drowning. I believe I can reach her. Yes!

"Hold on, I'll get to you. I'll help get you to the shore!"

"There, your feet can touch the sand. Hold on to me and I'll help, you make it to the beach."

"Oh, thank you. I was swimming and got this terrible cramp. Thank you for being my savior."

"Glad I was there. Can I help you get home?"

"Oh, I don't want to put you out any more. I believe that I can make it now."

"Why were you swimming so late in the evening? And alone?"

"I love to swim, particularly in the ocean, the gentle waves caressing me, and the evening is the best time of day for swimming. Also, it helps me sleep. I always swim alone. What's your name? You saved my life; I should at least know your name."

"My name is George. What's yours?"

"It's Elizabeth, but people call me Beth."

"Well I'm happy to know you, Beth, and I'm glad that I was there when you called."

"By the way, why were you there George? Are you an evening swimmer also?"

"Oh no, just out walking."

"Out walking in the water," she said with a smile.

"It doesn't really matter, does it? Do you live here in Florida year-round or only in the winter?"

"This is my home. How about you?"

"I spend summers in Maine but winter here in Pompano."

"That sounds interesting. What do you do in Maine?"

"The same thing I do here. I'm a writer."

"Oh! What do you write?"

"Mostly stories and articles for magazines. But let's not talk about me. Tell me about you."

"I'm a divorcee. I help out at the local library and occasionally at the school as a volunteer. A rather dull life, I'm afraid."

"Are you in a relationship, Beth? Anyone regular?"

"No, George. Are you?"

"Not at the moment. Perhaps we could celebrate your escape from the ocean by going to dinner sometime soon."

"That would be great! Did you remember that tomorrow is February fourteenth? We could celebrate Valentine's Day with a nice dinner."

"What a nice valentine that would be."

The Optimist

—◆—

Oh to see worthiness in all things.
To see the glass with drink remaining.
How easy life would be if all problems
Could be viewed as opportunities;
Each morn greeted with expectant joy,
Each day viewed with anticipation,
Each eve celebrated with success;
Each night to be filled with perfect dreams.
When life offers those bitter lemons;
How great to add a bit of sugar,
Share sweet nectar with a joyful friend,
Never tasting bitterness offered.
What joy to hear only harmony,
And to strain out the discordant noise;
To sing with joyful abandonment
And worry not to offend an ear.

The Interview

———

HE CAREFULLY BACKED OUT OF his drive and drove down the street. After stopping at the stop sign and looking both ways, he carefully pulled out onto the highway and drove sedately toward town. He reached the office complex at ten of ten and parked exactly and squarely between the yellow lines in the parking lot. After all, this was extremely important; he had been invited to his first job interview in almost a year.

The receptionist smiled pleasantly as she invited him to take a chair while she quietly called someone from her desk phone. He had barely sat down before a sandy-haired man dressed in a blue suit with a red-and-blue striped tie appeared and spoke to him by name.

"My name is Frank White," the man said as he thrust out his hand. "Thank you for agreeing to come and see us. Please come and meet Susan, my co-worker." He led the way into a hallway that eventually brought them into a small conference room with a table and six chairs. One chair was occupied by an attractive, dark-haired woman, who was also dressed in a dark blue suit with a white blouse.

"Susan Ferman, this is Elwin Stout. Elwin, Susan."

She stood and offered her hand with a friendly smile. "Very pleased to meet you, Elwin," she said.

"It's nice to meet you also, Susan," he responded.

Frank indicated a chair on the other side of the table from Susan, and then took a chair beside her. After some brief small talk: comments about the weather, local ball teams, pleasant surroundings, and such, the two interviewers asked several questions and explained the nature of the position that was open. Elwin queried the details of the company and ended with a request concerning the remaining interview process.

Frank and Susan then said, "We will escort you to the office of the vice president who would like to have a few words with you, and then you'll be free to return home. Assuming everyone who has met you is in agreement, you will be invited to meet the president, and final details will be resolved. We can tell you that we are very impressed with how well your résumé and answers today match with our needs. We are certainly hopeful that we have answered all of your questions concerning out mission and operations."

The vice president spent several minutes stressing the importance of the company in milieu of this particular business and how vital this job was in achieving the corporate goals.

After his meeting with the vice president, Elwin returned to the parking lot and retrieved his car. He carefully drove himself home. He was quite aware that the traffic was very bad and people drove recklessly. Having spent nearly a year unemployed, he was extremely careful with any expenses and especially his car, which would be required to take him to and from his employment if he obtained a job.

Two days later, he received a call from the company asking if he would be available to meet with the president for lunch on Friday at one. He immediately agreed.

Again dressed in his dark suit with a white shirt and tie, he departed for his luncheon date with plenty of time to spare. Recognizing that he was quite nervous, he drove more carefully than ever, never leaving the right-hand lane. Cars regularly whizzed by him. As he approached the turn to leave the main highway, half a mile yet from his destination, he slowed nearly to a stop and carefully negotiated the turn. The driver behind him finally lost patience and attempted to pass him while making the same turn. In doing so, he clipped Elwin's left front fender with his rear bumper. Elwin was livid! Not only has his car been damaged, but this accident was going to make him late for his appointment.

He pulled to the right curb and jumped out of his car. The other driver, a young man obviously still in his teens, had gone a further twenty or thirty feet before parking. Elwin looked with dismay at his crumpled fender, and then glanced up as the youth approached.

"What is the matter with you, trying to pass on a corner?" Elwin tried to maintain some semblance of calm but was finding it difficult.

"Well, why were you stopping right on the corner?" the young man retaliated. "You shouldn't even be driving the way you're holding up traffic."

"Listen, young man, I've been driving for many years and know enough to use caution when rounding a curve. Your recklessness has caused damage to my car and is going to make me late for an important meeting. Do you even have a license?"

"I've got a license, old man! How about you? Sure they haven't taken yours away?"

"Listen you young whippersnapper, show me your license and registration while I call a policeman."

"I've got a license and registration. Show me yours!"

By now a few people had gathered to enjoy the sideshow. Elwin had fumbled out his telephone and punched in 911, but a passing police officer, noticing the melee, had already arrived.

"OK, folks. Let's cool down and figure out what happened, here," the patrol officer said.

"It's plain what happened, this young kid tried to pass me as I was making this turn and he damaged my car."

"The old man had stopped right on the corner so I went around him but he began moving again and caused me to catch my bumper on his fender."

"I did not stop, I took the turn cautiously!" retorted Elwin.

"Wait a minute! You," indicating the youth—"go sit in your car and find your driver's license and registration."

"You!"—he indicated Elwin—"get your license and registration, and then calmly tell me what you did and how the accident happened."

Elwin found his license and registration and handed them to the police officer. While the patrol officer noted the information, Elwin called the company and explained that he would be a few minutes late due to an automobile accident.

"Now, you wait right here until I get the information from the other party, and then I'll let you go on."

"But, I have a very important meeting that I am already late for," Elwin complained.

"Sorry about your meeting, but you'll need the other information for your insurance company, so wait right here."

Eventually, the patrol officer finished with the young man and sent him along while he walked back to Elwin's car and handed him the necessary paperwork. Elwin was then allowed to proceed, and he cautiously, but a bit more expeditiously, drove on to his appointment.

After parking his car in the lot, he entered the building. The same pleasant receptionist welcomed him and immediately picked up the telephone to announce his arrival. A gracious woman of approximately fifty with very attractive silver hair appeared and invited Elwin to follow her. They entered an elevator, rose to the second floor, and proceeded down the corridor to what appeared to be a reception room for a corner office. He was invited to take a chair for a few moments. "The president was inadvertently interrupted by his son, a most unusual occurrence."

"Do you have any children, Mr. Stout?" asked the receptionist.

"Yes, I have two, a girl, twelve, and a boy, ten," he answered.

"I suspect then that you have not faced the difficulties of a teenager yet, Mr. Stout. Those are difficult years for parents as well as children."

The door to the inner office opened, and, to my horror, my nemesis of reckless driving appeared.

Made in the USA
Middletown, DE
07 June 2016